NE Free Public Library
NEW HAVEN, CONN.

D0679232

SE 2 8

OCT 11 19

DEC 2 8 1984

JAN 1 1 1985

OCT 1 2 1985

AUG 1 2 1987

SEP 6 1988

DEC 3 1986

FEB 1 6 199

FEB 1 3 199

SEP 1 5 19

MA

AUG 2 4 19

FORM

THE SPEECH WRITING GUIDE

WILEY SERIES ON HUMAN COMMUNICATION

W. A. Mambert
PRESENTING TECHNICAL IDEAS: A Guide to Audience Communication

William J. Bowman
GRAPHIC COMMUNICATION

Herman M. Weisman
*TECHNICAL CORRESPONDENCE: A Handbook and Reference Source
for the Technical Professional*

John H. Mitchell
WRITING FOR TECHNICAL AND PROFESSIONAL JOURNALS

James J. Welsh
*THE SPEECH WRITING GUIDE: Professional Techniques for Regular and
Occasional Speakers*

Michael P. Jaquish
PERSONAL RESUMÉ PREPARATION

George T. Vardaman and Carroll C. Halterman
*COMMUNICATION FOR MANAGERIAL CONTROL: Systems for Organizational
Diagnosis and Design*

John D. Haughney
EFFECTIVE CATALOGS

THE SPEECH
WRITING GUIDE

Professional Techniques for
Regular and Occasional Speakers

JAMES J. WELSH

Director of Creative Services
E. R. Squibb & Sons, Inc.

FREE PUBLIC
LIBRARY
NEW HAVEN CT

JOHN WILEY & SONS, INC., NEW YORK · LONDON · SYDNEY

FREE PUBLIC
LIBRARY
NEW WEB

Copyright © 1968 by John Wiley & Sons, Inc.

All rights reserved.
No part of this book may be reproduced by any means,
nor transmitted, nor translated into a machine language
without the written permission of the publisher.

Library of Congress Catalog Card Number: 68-19782
GB 471 93359X
Printed in the United States of America

To Judy

PREFACE

I have written this book as a guide for the professional men of business, science, and engineering who are regular speakers and for those who are required to make only an occasional speech. Essentially, it is intended as a practical reference tool for writing a worthwhile speech—a speech noted for clarity, unity, and economy and one that has something to say to an audience. Guides for speech delivery are also included.

Fundamental guides to speech writing are presented in Part I; ten chapters in that part also have check lists that contain key review points for quick and precise comparison of the writing with the suggested guides.

Part II, titled "Reference," contains guides, suggestions, and specialized information that supplement the techniques of speech writing. Part III is a directory of information sources.

James J. Welsh

New York, N.Y.
March 1968

CONTENTS

THE SPEECH WRITING GUIDE

PART I

GUIDES TO SPEECH WRITING

1

THE NEED FOR A GUIDE

Both the regular and the occasional speechmaker can find something of value in these remarks:

"Yet, with all the work, skill, thought, planning, and time that go into the executive speech, Opinion Research (Corporation) found . . . that only 28 per cent measure up as really good. More than half scored as dull, banal, or obvious."

Those of us who are regular speech writers and speechmakers may be irritated by the results of the above survey. Worse yet, we might assume that it is "the other fellow" whose speech is in the banal majority. The occasional speech writer is implicitly cautioned to strive for a "really good" speech.

It is reasonable to assume that poor speech writing is, at least, one principal cause for poor speechmaking. This small book attempts to help both the regular speaker and writer compose, in the fullest sense of the word, worthwhile speeches. It is also intended to point the way for the occasional speaker, who will use it as a model and consult it as a guide.

When you are asked to make a speech, you are being asked to communicate. Communication is the civilized battle today, tomorrow, and in the future. How you communicate is the strategic plan of business and community life—for you and your company.

Whatever your personal reaction to the work of preparing a speech, the impersonal effects of a speech tell on you. The speech indicates your abilities; it establishes a reputation; it provides a step for future advancement.

SPEECH WRITING IN PERSPECTIVE

Some fundamental information about speeches and speech writing in general may add perspective to the business of writing.

Writing a speech calls for skill, art, and craft. The smooth blending of these elements is never an easy task, but there are guides and techniques—shortcuts—to make composition easier. The novice speech writer and the versatile professional both use, or need to use, skill, art, and craft. The experienced writer is at ease with those fundamentals. He enjoys self-confidence because he has grown in his work. However, speech writing is still hard work for the professional.

Assume that you are competent in your own specialty—science, engineering, or business. With diligent application you can write a speech that is interesting, informative, and satisfying to your audience. You might, on occasion, use those same adjectives yourself.

You may be asked to speak on a subject that is only remotely connected with your expertise. A present trend of thought seems to hold that if you are a "specialist" you ought to be able to tackle almost any field related to your competency.

Just recently an executive was booked as a speaker at a meeting of the Federal Government's Accountants' Association. The speech topic assigned to him was "Evolving Techniques for Financial Control." The Association, numbering 3000 members, was a mixture of computer experts, EDP specialists and, of course, accounting professionals.

The executive's understanding of his formidable topic, and his familiarity with the work of the Association's members, was based on the slender thread of his company's manufacturing metal housings for electronic equipment and office furniture.

With some professional help—he did have some solid ideas on the subject—he found his speech quoted in the *Wall Street Journal*.

The audience that comes to hear a speaker today is better educated, more sophisticated, and more demanding. Many of your listeners have been speakers. Some are experienced speechmakers. All expect the speaker to say something worthwhile. They expect to be informed. It would seem that they have a *right* to hear a good speech.

Recently, one experienced speech writer made the comment that fully 80 per cent of today's speeches are boring. He observed further that speakers have little to say, and what they do say is said poorly.

Is this business of speech writing important? During a business year, it is conservatively estimated that about 50,000 formal speeches are given in the United States. If the future of our civilization holds anything, it holds an ever-increasing demand for communications.

Also the speech is a tool for advancement. In a nationwide poll of top management, conducted by *Harvard Business Review* and published in April 1964, the executives were asked to list the traits most important for a future executive. The survey showed this striking result: "The single most important trait for an executive is the ability to communicate." No other trait was even close.

2
WHAT IS A SPEECH?

This question probably has as many answers as there are speakers. Definitions might range from the simple "just a talk" to elaborate descriptions of Ciceronian and Churchillian elegance.

A speech, in one of its simplest definitions, is "a projected conversation." This interpretation may cause some concern, especially to the executive who has composed a few speeches. Properly understood, however, the definition is helpful to the executive speech writer.

"Conversation" means that the tone, the manner, and the approach in writing should reflect the same ease in conversation that a person enjoys in talking about his hobby, his favorite pro football team, or certain aspects of his work. The tenor of the writing should be at the conversational level.

THE LANGUAGE OF CONVERSATION

Writing a speech at the conversational level does not mean, of course, that the language of conversation—cryptic, obscure, and contradictory—should be used in your speech. Here is an example that clearly shows why the language of conversation is useless:

(A): Did you tell him about the increased budget for. . . .
(B): Yes, he said he knew about it earlier, and he would, you know. . . .
(A): But did he get the approval on the last section of the. . . .
(B): No, he was told by John that this could be. . . .
(A): Will you see him tomorrow?

(B): Yes, and I'll ask him about . . . incidentally, first quarter
        sales for his department. . . .
(A): Yes, I heard.

This conversation had a meaning to the speakers because so much
had been previously understood by them. This is not true for a speech
where your audience hears a formal talk for the first time.

To say that a speech is "projected conversation" means that the
speaker gives his information before an audience, gathered specifically
to hear him talk. The conversation is broadcast to an entire assembly.

Both elements of this definition are important because they help the
speaker to transfer from the natural, informal, enjoyable circumstances of a conversation to circumstances that are unnatural (a
strange environment), formal (a consistent quality of speech), and
enjoyable (perhaps only after the speech has been delivered).

"SPEECHIFYING IS A DIFFERENT ANIMAL"

Frequently, educated people interpret verbal and journalistic skills
as speech writing skills. To many of these people, a speech is a prose
composition, written with an eye toward publication. The writing may
be excellent, but it will probably be a poor speech.

The speech writer should bear in mind that a speech is to be heard;
a speech is to be understood.

The complicated, involved sentence structure of the periodic style,
a dependency on verbiage, and the use of a sesquipedalian vocabulary
(as this very sentence shows), are very difficult to listen to, difficult to
retain, and hard to understand.

In written work the reader has the opportunity to read again and
again until he can extract the meaning. On the other hand, the listener
to a speech finds that one syllable gives way to the next, and that
grasping the speaker's thoughts and putting them together in context is
a nebulous and elusive activity.

A top speech writer made this remark as a guide to one of his journalistic associates: "Speechifying is a different animal." And the statement is easily proved. The speech that first appears to be simple, repetitive, and almost naïve in content and composition will usually turn
out to be a fine speech.

It is extremely important to discard preconceived notions on the nature of a speech. The ease with which the executive composes his speech, the logic and orderliness of his treatment, and his effectiveness on the audience are directly related to his ideas on what makes a speech. In effect, those notions are translated into "How I think a speech should be written."

Some men have converted excellent compositions into excellent speeches. Men like MacArthur . . . Churchill . . . Stevenson.

And yet the speech writing executive must develop and master techniques of composition. He must also acquire some skill as a public speaker.

3

IMPORTANCE OF
REFERENCE MATERIAL

Professional speech writers estimate that the work of speech writing is reduced 25 to 50 per cent if copious reference material is available.

The "first-time" speech writer and also the comparatively inexperienced writer should gather numerous reference sources, should read the sources thoroughly, and should base the speech outline on the final selection of reference material. Don't be shy, don't be afraid, don't be proud in borrowing information; your originality will show in your treatment of the facts. The sources may be newspapers, magazines, journals, or professional association feature articles.

Knowing that reference material is needed is a good sign; getting the material may be difficult. Part III of this book, "Directory of Information Sources," has 45 general headings under which government, business, science, and industrial information sources are listed by name and address. Each of these contacts is a direct lead to reference material. Of course, the speech writer also has local information channels, such as chambers of commerce, libraries, and newspaper files.

The speech writer may ask, "How much reference material do I need?" He should trust his own prudential judgment. As a rule he should collect five to ten times more material than he thinks he needs to write the speech. This is only a loose guide; the job at hand is writing the speech, and too much time in microscopic research may mean too little time for writing.

4

USING A SPEECH WRITER

This chapter may seem out of place in a book whose purpose is to help a person write his *own* speech. But a great many companies do use speech writers today. Therefore, some reasons for this use and a description of speech writing services are appropriate here.

These comments are primarily intended for that audience of several hundred thousand professionals who are called executives, and who use speech writers. However, the information given here should be of interest to that much larger group of professionals, in both line and service operations, who form the middle-management ranks. Eventually many people from that group will be in need of speech writers.

THE PROFESSIONAL SPEECH WRITER

The professional speech writer may come from an advertising or public relations agency; he may be free-lance; or he may be a "moonlighter." If he came from an advertising or public relations agency or works free-lance, speech writing is but one specialty of a full-time occupation: writing. If he is a "moonlighter," he has a full-time occupation other than speech writing, but takes assignments as a personal service, or to supplement his income, or for other reasons.

Any one of these three types may be retained by a company, depending on the writer's qualifications and the cost of his services.

BENEFITS THAT A COMPANY RECEIVES

There are three benefits that a speech writer can offer a company: talent, counsel, and time. My explanation of these three concepts shows why a company retains a professional speech writer.

The *talent* of the speech writer is that of a specialist. His training, experience, and occupation are all centered on writing; his credentials may include hundreds of speeches. He will be skilled in the techniques of writing and the subtleties of language.

The professional speech writer will be able to *counsel* the executive on the effects of certain phrasing, on the impact of speech, or to suggest slanting the viewpoint toward a certain group, and to give other ideas. The truly professional speech writer will offer more than writing techniques.

The company retaining a speech writer also buys *time*. The senior executive usually cannot afford to devote his time to speech writing; the speech writer can. The speech writer will work all night on a speech—he can afford to. The executive cannot—not if he is going to deliver the speech the next day or put in a day's work at the office. The speech writer can spend days in researching material; the executive cannot afford that time, but he can afford to use the writer.

EFFECTIVE USE OF A SPEECH WRITER

The speech writer will not turn out a good speech unless the executive helps him. For this purpose the executive should schedule a brief planning session (15 to 20 minutes) with the writer. The executive should discuss the speech topic and the particular aspect of it that is to be stressed, certain ideas that he wants in the speech, and concepts that he does not want included. He should set the review-draft and final-speech deadlines. He should also give some leads on research sources: the organization requesting the speech, company personnel, a magazine feature story, and any other material that may be of help to the writer.

COST OF SERVICES

Generally, the cost of a speech ranges from $500 to $2500. Agency and individual charges vary. Some speech writers charge on a flat-fee-per-speech basis; others apply a rate of $20 to $50 an hour in pricing the speech.

EVALUATING THE SPEECH WRITER'S SPEECH

Certainly no executive should blindly accept the work of a speech writer just because he is a speech writer. Some writers are excellent, many do "average" work, some turn out a poor product. This book will help the executive to judge the quality of writing received; Chapter 7, titled "Writing a Lean Speech," and Chapter 12, "As You Write," may help get better performance from the speech writer.

5

ADVANCE AUDIENCE ANALYSIS

The title of this chapter has no Freudian overtones. "Advance audience analysis" simply means learning as much as possible about the audience who will hear the speech, and incorporating that knowledge into the speech. At first glance it may seem annoyingly obvious to recommend that a speaker analyze and evaluate his prospective audience. But that is "surface analysis"; what is suggested here is an indepth penetration of the heart of the audience—in short, their reason for existence as an audience.

In using advance audience analysis, the speechmaker attempts to learn something about the plans, programs, problems, and peculiarities of his specialized audience. He learns and uses some of the specialized terms that his audience regularly uses. He finds out and alludes to trends in the discipline of the audience; he refers to the thinking that is prevalent in the audience, and adopts it to his speech.

VALUE OF ADVANCE ANALYSIS

The use of advance analysis brings added value to the speaker, the speech, and the audience. This in-depth analysis makes a case for the speaker with his audience. After all, his speech benefits because it talks the language of the audience. It does, indeed, show that he took pains in the preparation, that he made an extra effort to identify with the needs of his audience, and that he does, in some measure, know what he is talking about to that specialized audience.

The probability of audience receptivity is greatly increased; the allusions to the thoughts, trends, and terminology of the group become rungs on the ladder of the speech, by which the audience can follow the ideas of the speaker. And it permits a fairly easy transition from the unique thoughts of the speaker to the unique knowledge of the audience.

If my previous remarks seem to be in the abstract, the following detailed example of advance audience analysis should reduce the discussion to the practical working level.

ANALYSIS IN ACTION

I shall use one of my own speeches as an example—not because the speech is meritorious but because the circumstances of the speech furnish an ideal model for explaining advance audience analysis. I was asked to talk to a large audience of data-processing experts. My knowledge of computers and computer applications is extremely limited. But, in my search for background information and in my readings and discussions on the subject, I found that the following specialized language was recognized as current and meaningful, and was adaptable to my speech.

(1). *Real Time.* Computer language for information immediately available from the computer, as opposed to data stored for later use.

(2). *Exception Information.* Using only the information that calls for action decisions, while avoiding routine information.

(3). *Total System.* A system by which all the information functions of a large company are handled by electronic data processing.

(4). *Third Generation Computers.* The present advance machines as opposed to the early models, and the first large use of standardized production models.

(5). *Software.* Manuals of instruction for converting data in the various languages of computers.

Some sentences taken from my speech show how advance analysis is adapted to, and identified with, the specialized audience:

> (1). We need some *real time*—some immediate planning—to improve our office arrangements, our data gathering, our work flow to the computer.

(2). Must an executive wade through stacks of documents before making a decision? . . . Management can read *exception information* retrieved from a computer operating a mile from the executive office.

(3). The systems men are busy planning a *Total System,* one that will handle all the data communications of a complex corporation.

(4 and 5). I'm sure you are aware of some of the problems of this *Third Generation* of computers. . . . *software development* is very slow.

SOURCES OF INFORMATION

The two sources for material for advance audience analysis are research and personal contact.

The sources for research are the publications of the association, such as annual reports, monthly journals or bulletins, and the trade press—the specialty magazines. The national business magazines (*Time, Forbes, U. S. News, Business Week*) can be excellent sources on almost every major topic, from Medicare to miniskirts and from the Beatles to ballistics.

For up-to-the-minute information, personal contact (either by telephone or face-to-face) is the best source of information. In this way specific questions and ideas of the speechmaker can be resolved in a way that few written articles can offer. Program chairmen, directors of associations, and public relations directors are first-hand and accurate sources and can provide helpful tips to the speaker.

It has been my experience that these individuals are glad to help, and will provide the speechmaker with information and the ways to interpret it.

There is some mutual back-scratching involved; the success of an organization's program depends on the success of the speaker or speakers. The speaker wants to do a good job. The sponsoring group wants him to do a good job. Therefore, the inquiring speechmaker will usually get plenty of information.

THINGS TO AVOID

Two things should be avoided in using advance audience analysis: (1) trying to sound like an expert in the field, and (2) trying to construct a speech based exclusively on identity with the audience's expertise.

In using advance audience analysis, the speaker is trying to establish some common bonds, some identity between himself and his audience. The idea is to make use of their language to help put his idea across, and to make them understand his point of view. What the speaker should offer is a different view point on an idea that is understood in one way by his listeners. He alludes to a new interpretation or a new slant on an "old" idea. This is legitimate and is understood and appreciated by the audience.

Trying to build a speech based exclusively on identity with the audience's competency might work, but I think that the result would be a debacle for several reasons. First, the audience does not want to hear what it knows already. In all probability they are expecting a fresh approach to a problem, some suggestions, or some challenges to their own comfortable routines.

They want to hear what *you* have to offer them. Quite properly they expect you to tell them to set their sights a notch higher. The speech should contain a sprinkling of the speaker's general knowledge of his audience. The judicious use of advance audience analysis will depend in great measure on common sense.

6

THE SPEECH OUTLINE

A useful tool for speech writing is the outline. It should be a well thought out, carefully constructed framework that defines the limits of a speech topic. For the neophyte speech writer the outline is imperative. For the experienced writer it is indispensable.

The purpose of an outline is to organize and channel thoughts along a central theme. The outline helps the writer to stick to the point and, in so doing, to assemble a cohesive speech. The speech outline gives "the big picture" of the subject range, permits a critical analysis of defects and strong points in the speech framework, and serves as a concise summary of speech highlights. The outline is essential for delivering nonmemorized talks and for avoiding word-for-word speeches read to an audience.

A well-constructed outline aids the speaker in an emergency. Frequently, a speaker is asked to pare his speech when other program speakers have disrupted the time schedule. The outline permits the speaker to lengthen or shorten his talk with little effort. More important, he can still make a good speech.

THE OUTLINE SAVES TIME

The speech writer will find that the outline is a generator of thought. First, the writer is forced to list a number of points relating to the theme. Thought must be given to each item listed; without an outline, the first good idea that developed would probably receive all of the concentration.

Too often (much too often) a person will say, "I have to write a speech," and will promptly sit down and begin writing it. In this case the purely physical and mechanical skills of writing the speech are considered to be the same as composing (writing) a speech. This defect seems to indicate acting before thinking.

There are two major elements absolutely essential to every good speech: the speech outline and speech research. The speech-research topic was discussed earlier.

If an outline is prepared, about one-third of the work of speech writing is done. If the outline has been written, writing the full speech will be a comparatively easy task. With a good outline before him, the executive speech writer knows what has to be said, in what order it has to be said, how his theme and subthemes must be supported, and what additional information he needs to turn out a finished product.

STARTING AN OUTLINE

How is an outline started? I suggest one method that has proved useful, and gets the outline off to a quick start. This method saves time, which, in speech writing, is frequently of the essence.

Take a sheet of lined paper. Jot down every thought that comes into your head regarding the speech title assigned.

As you write down each thought on the speech, skip about four lines between each idea written down. When you think you've exhausted the list of things you want to say, stop. Now, review the ideas.

At this point the chances are quite good that you have included not only the structural members for building the outline but subtopics and some supporting arguments as well. You will certainly have additional thoughts as you finish the outline, but it is now possible to rearrange the written ideas into a working form.

One of the chief difficulties in writing a speech without an outline is that you will find (and can prove this for yourself) that all kinds of seemingly unrelated thoughts keep popping into your mind as you are writing. These ideas *do* pertain to the speech, but not at that point at which you are currently writing.

If you follow this note-jotting technique in preparing the outline, you will be quite pleased to discover that you seem to know more and have more to say than you thought you did before starting your notes.

SUMMARY CHECK LIST

Sample Outline

Topic: *"Automobile Safety"*

SECTION 1.   REVIEW OF CURRENT NEWS

1.1 Comments of Nader's book
1.2 Testimony of auto experts
1.3 Detroit's reaction

1.1 *Nader's "Unsafe at Any Speed"*
—background on author
—examples in book: selective, slanted, sensational
—engineering qualifications of author

1.2 *Testimony of Experts*
—engineering directors of "Big Three"
—safety tests used: brake, impact, suspension

1.3 *Detroit's Reactions*
—discussion with government agency
—compliance with standards, generally
—will increase cost to consumer

7

WRITING A LEAN SPEECH

The speeches of professional men who are nonwriters generally share one common fault: wordiness. This defect applies to both the length of the speech and to the composition of each sentence. When the speech draft is given a final editing, emphasis is placed on content, and little notice is given to the words. This oversight probably arises from a lack of familiarity with speech writing techniques and from too much familiarity with the English language.

Many speeches are undisciplined compositions. Undisciplined writing results from the failure to criticize the single common denominator of every sentence: the word. Strangely enough, the undisciplined writer can usually pour out a flood of words and ideas. His words are a rich source of material; his failure to refine the material vitiates his thoughts.

"BEATING AROUND THE BUSH"

The uncritical speech writer is guilty of "beating around the bush"; he turns out a product that contains detrimental fat—detrimental to thought, detrimental to action, and detrimental to the audience. This sentence shows the "fat" of undisciplined writing: "He was diagnosed as being afflicted with cancer." There are some nice 25-cent words in the sentence—"diagnosed," "afflicted"—but how much greater the impact would be in the use of three simple words, "He had cancer." In the first example eight words are used. But three words are enough.

In the first sentence the audience must listen to and remember two concepts ("He was diagnosed" and "being afflicted") before it can grasp the main idea: He had cancer. The action of the sentence is slowed down by the hurdles placed before the "impact concept." The impact concept is the one word, the one idea, that clearly states the speech writer's thought, and that has impact on the audience.

Another example will demonstrate the effect of undisciplined writing: ". . . as reported in one of the special magazines which deals with the chemical industry." Of the 14 words in this example 8 are monosyllables with no action—for instance, "of," "in," and "the." The audience must notice each of the nonimpact words; the listeners' minds must figuratively trim off the fat that surrounds the central thought. How much more impact the words would have had and how much kinder the speech writer would have been to the audience if he had stated, "A chemical magazine reports. . . ."

One or two instances of undisciplined writing may not affect either the speech or the audience. But a 20-minute speech filled with this kind of writing can cause adverse audience reaction. Generally, undisciplined speeches can be compressed to 70 per cent of the original volume—with some increase in favorable reception by the listeners.

Wordiness is only one possible failing for the speech writer. Other failings are redundancy, "adjectivitis," circumlocution, the use of the abstract for the concrete, and the writing of "nothing" sentences.

The journalistic sins of the speech writer are comparatively easy to detect in the writings of others. The speech writer has certain blind spots as he writes. When he can bring cold criticism to his work and can accept the critical comments of others, his writing will be disciplined.

REDUNDANCY

Redundancy is the unconscious skill of saying the same thing twice in different ways in the same expression. Deliberate redundancy is a rhetorical device, and its occasional use can be justified. Unconscious redundancy clutters up the speech and displays careless composition.

The executive who wrote a memo stating, "The management newsletter will be distributed every Friday of every week" received a few critical memos in return. If the memo is distributed every Friday, it must come out every week.

The guest speaker who said that he was going to quote an "old adage" just got careless; an "adage" is an "old" saying. The drug executive who said that his products were prepared in plants of "spotless purity" certainly never saw "dirty purity."

ADJECTIVES ARE FRIENDS

"Adjectivitis" is a term that I coined to define a writing technique that calls for the use of adjectives wherever possible. Someone has said that "adjectives should be the friends of nouns." The indiscriminate use of adjectives weakens the nouns' meaning and detracts from the force of words. This is an unnatural device, and one that an audience quickly notices in a speech.

The device is unnatural because it is against the very nature of things. A qualifying element, such as an adjective, calls special attention to the noun concept. If the speech writer sows adjectives willy-nilly, he indicates a lack of judgment and balance in evaluating concepts. Adjectivitis is unnatural because it runs counter to human nature; the speaker's remarks can be qualified other than adjectivally, but if his material is factual, it can be stated in black and white terms. Adjectives are the friends of nouns; indiscriminate friendship is disastrous to a speech.

Some instances of adjectivitis are: "considerable skill"—you either have skill or you haven't; "small dot"—ever see a big dot? And the classic examples are: "a little bit pregnant"—a minor miracle; "written signature"—how else can you get a signature except by writing it?; "this new improvement"—can there be an "old improvement?"; or a "personal vendetta"—a vendetta is directed against someone by a person seeking revenge.

THE "NOTHING" SENTENCE

The "nothing" sentence is one that really contributes nothing to the factual content of the speech. It creates a hiatus in the thought process and leaves an audience wondering what was meant by the words.

Nothing sentences are very common in all professional writings— in electronics, chemistry, physics, and general business. The hallmark of the nothing sentence is that the listener or reader captures the thought of the statement, agrees, and then is puzzled as to why he agreed.

Next time you take an elevator in a public building, look at the license and read what it says. Usually the words read like this: "It is unlawful to operate this elevator unless this card is displayed in it." What happens when the card is removed? How does that statement benefit anyone, either inside or outside the elevator?

The transportation executive who issued the edict, "The emergency keys are not to be used for any purpose whatsoever," undoubtedly knew what he wanted to say, and he wanted to add emphasis to an annoying situation. But the obvious rejoinder to his statement is, "When are emergency keys used?"

When a speech writer states "Congressional legislation will ensure a substantial order of improvement in welfare programs and administration"—and lets it go at that—the writer has fashioned a nothing sentence. The bland statement regarding substantial improvement causes questions to arise that demand factual answers. What does substantial improvement of program mean, and how is welfare administration improved?

The critical speech writer might handle that zero statement in this way: "Congressional legislation will ensure a substantial improvement in welfare programs in three key areas: cash payments to the poor, free prescription drugs, and visiting nurse service."

In the preceding example, something specific, concrete, and factual has been stated. Now the speech writer can expand on each of those three meaningful topics. And he will have something to say to his audience. Nothing sentences are frequently nothing more than journalistic camouflage. The writer did not do his homework and the speech shows it.

An earlier warning to the executive speech writer is appropriate here: "Speechifying is a different animal." The speech is not meant to be a feature article for publication. The sentences must be precise, factual, and straightforward—so much so that they seem to be oversimplified, plain, and naked prose. This is what the journalist calls "tight writing"; that is, as lean as the writer can make it. Then the audience can easily follow and clearly understand.

In Section 2 of Part II, "Reference," we shall examine three pages of exercises containing all of the careless writing habits discussed here. This will be interesting editorial practice for a speech writer. Also in Part II there are corrected versions and critical comment on the exercises.

SUMMARY CHECK LIST

Trim all verbal fat

Eliminate "nothing" sentences

Use concrete terms

Write tight sentences

Justify adjectives

8

WATCH YOUR LANGUAGE

This chapter on language and Chapter 10 on style are so closely related that some overlapping in content occurs. Under the heading of language comes vocabulary, "suffixitis," and quotations.

For any speech writer the general rule on vocabulary should be: use the words you need to make your meaning clear. A common failing among occasional speech writers is the use of big words for the sake of big words. This fault is common with college sophomores, and is frequently called "sophomoric writing." Words are used simply to display the scope of vocabulary. The Summary Check List at the end of this section shows a few of the blatant examples of "worditis." These examples bear a close relation to euphemism, which substitutes "passed away" for "died."

Remember the general rule of thumb: use the words you need to make the meaning clear. Writers commonly refer to words as nickel and quarter words. Both types are legitimate, necessary, and obviously useful. The application of these words is the downfall of the inexperienced writer.

"He had an appendectomy" is preferred to the expression "He had his appendix taken out" or "He was operated on for appendicitis." "Appendectomy" is a 25-cent word, but its use is clearly warranted. "Implosion" is preferred to "exploded inward"; "asphyxiated" is preferred to the incorrect "he choked to death"; and "reneged" is preferable to "he went back on his word." The 25-cent words are needed in writing.

However, the writer should learn to use little words—the 5-cent kind—in his speech. Actually, it is much more important that the speech writer make use of small words: his audience can grasp his thoughts much easier.

The professional worker—scientist, engineer, chemist—should avoid several pitfalls peculiar to persons who specialize in a discipline. These pitfalls are jargon, suffixitis, and "technicalese."

JARGON

Jargon is really nothing more than shop talk. It is a specialized vocabulary that permits workers to communicate rapidly, effectively, and precisely. It is an important tool at work. Jargon is out of place in a speech. Its use may even make the speaker seem ludicrous.

Fowler * defines jargon as "talk that is considered both ugly sounding and hard to understand." Some examples from the worlds of government, business, education, and science should prove amusing and instructive.

Government

| "Overkill" | We will kill you at least once; very mean |
| "Tactical nuclear exchange" | East and West H-bomb one another |

Education

| "Culturally enriched core curriculum" | Untranslatable |
| "Good socio-oriented life skills" | Doesn't beat-up the other kids |

Science

| The "hard" sciences | Very technical as opposed to less technical; physics and mathematics versus biology and philosophy. Doesn't mean easy subject versus "tough" subject |

Business

| A real gem from the stock market: "Emphasis toward growth-oriented equities selling at reasonable appraisals of foreseeable earnings" | Take a prudent risk on investing |

* *A Dictionary of Modern Usage,* cited in Section 7 of Part II.

If jargon is absolutely necessary to your speech, an explanation of the term should be given to the audience the first time the term is used. Generally, jargon should be avoided.

In the use of a technical term, the speech writer should clearly explain the meaning for the audience. For example, if an aircraft manufacturer speaks to the Rotary Club or the Chamber of Commerce on "general aviation," he is using a term that is technical to his industry; he is not talking about aviation in general or commercial airlines.

A WORD TO THE WISE

"Suffixitis" is a disease now reaching the epidemic stage. The only symptom of this malady is the use of the word "wise" tacked onto the end of a word—any word—to make an instant adverb or replace a phrase.

We read it in magazines, hear it at work, hear it on radio and TV —in fact, the disease is everywhere.

Weatherwise, the week end looks like . . . Trafficwise, the situation is . . . Costwise, the budget is . . . Travelwise, all arrangements are . . . and the examples could go on and on.

Where this practice originated is hard to track down; I think it started in the large defense engineering companies. These establishments seem to be the breeding ground for these spectacular innovations. The extreme is typified in the story of the mother owl who asked her son's tutor how the little boy-owl was doing in school, "Wise-wise, that is."

The suffix may someday become an important and respected part of the language. There is much utility to it; it is succinct, expressive, and clear. Currently, it is also incorrect.

Englishwise, it does nothing for the language.

RUNNING TO BARTLETT'S

It is prudent to watch your language in using quotations. Recently, several speeches delivered by top executives in East Coast cities seemed to be miniatures of *Bartlett's Familiar Quotations.* One speech, 17 pages long, had 17 different quotations from as many people. Another speech of similar length had 23 quotes. Both speeches contained excellent ideas; the writers also had something new to say. But both speeches were severely criticized and properly so.

Each audience had expected the speaker to give *his* ideas, to give *his* viewpoints, and *his* opinions on the speech topic. The importance of the speech was lost because of this watering-down effect.

For the speech writer one or two quotations are usually sufficient. If the quote is appropriate to the speech topic, it can be skillfully used several times in the speech text.

No matter how good a number of quotations may seem to you, the speaker, they are still not you, and they are not your words. Your audience will be acutely conscious of that fact.

PRICE LIST OF WORDS

Quarter	Nickel
Compensation	Salary
Implementation	Start
Finalization	Completion
Rationale	Reason
Configuration	Arrangement
Optimum	Best
Launch vehicle	Rocket
Termination	Laid off
Disengaged	Fired
Disadvantaged	Poor
Cerebrating	Thinking
Utilization	Use

SUMMARY CHECK LIST

Eradicate "wise"
Use the appropriate word
Use small words
Avoid jargon
Minimize quotations

9

HUMOR IN A SPEECH

Many professional speech writers caution other speech writers to avoid any attempt at humor in a speech. Jokes and off-color remarks are considered to be taboo. But these same professionals start their own speeches with some favorite joke or anecdote. The use of humor in a speech is a touchy point. I favor the use of humor within the general framework of the suggestions given in this chapter.

The word "humor" does not mean "funny." Leave the funny remarks to the master of ceremonies. Being funny in a speech is a sure way to lose control of the audience. Don't tell jokes to start a speech. Assuming that your joke is genuinely funny, a number of people in the audience will have heard a better one and will try to tell it. Just a few distractions in the audience are enough to damage the speech's impact on the audience. Besides, how many are the speeches that start, "Speaking before this group today reminds me of the story of the traveling salesman who. . . ."

The humor that a speech writer may use should be determined while composing the speech. The definition of this type of humor is difficult; it should probably occur in that gray area between being pleasant and being funny. The remark may be humorous because of the way you deliver it, the way you smile as you make your comment, or the way you gesticulate. It may be just a quip or the gentle irony inherent in a particular sentence.

No writer can tell another writer how to be funny. What is offered in this chapter is opinion—experienced opinion—but still only opinion.

VALUE OF HUMOR

Humor in speeches is advantageous to the speaker and the audience. Humor helps relieve some of the artificial tension that exists in the speaker, in the audience, and in that intangible gap between speaker and audience. Humor helps to establish rapport with the listeners; it creates a bond between all participants, and it lets the audience see the human side of the speaker. The biographical notes on the speaker do not make him come alive for the audience. The one single trait that establishes him as another person to the audience is his humor.

How often should humor be used in a speech? Without counting preliminary remarks to the speech text, I suggest that two or three instances of humor in a 15- to 20-minute speech should be ample. Perhaps the prime function of speech humor is to provide a brief diversion from the subject matter. Ideally, there should be the tension of communication between speaker and audience, and some relaxing of this tension is mutually beneficial.

As for off-color and suggestive jokes and remarks, forget them. No matter how hard your audience laughs at "blue" humor, it is almost guaranteed that someone in your audience will be offended by it. And although that person may be one in a hundred, you have no idea who that one is—or what effect he may have on you.

If a Freudian slip occurs, make the best of the situation. A slip is a slip (no Freudian intended); usually, the audience will spontaneously get the speaker off an embarrassing hook; sometimes the speaker will need to prompt the audience to help him. From then on the audience will be on your side.

Before leaving the subject of humor, one suggestion: if you have a good joke to tell, make sure it is appropriate for your speech. Don't tell a joke simply because it is a good story.

SARCASM MEANS "RENDING FLESH"

The one thing that the audience will not forgive is sarcasm. Unless you have a group of frantic fanatics as your audience, don't use sarcasm. For some reason sarcasm leaves a bad taste in the mouth of the listener. Sarcasm seems to have the element of a vendetta against someone who is not present to defend his views. The sarcastic remark seems to ridicule a person by demeaning him for what he is instead of exposing his arguments or philosophy. It makes an otherwise effective speaker appear vicious. A speaker with something to say does not need sarcasm to present his convictions.

10

YOUR STYLE OF WRITING

There is the story of the college student who stood up in composition class one day and impatiently asked his teacher, "When are you going to teach us to write like Hemingway?"

The answer to that question is clear: no one can teach a writer to write like another author. An author's style can be imitated, for whatever that's worth. Imitative writing will be stillborn, sterile, and empty. Any writer, novice or professional, writes in his own style. That style may be described with any number of adjectives; one word, however, will always be used: original.

But a writer's style can reflect the *techniques of style* of another writer. His method of exposition, delineation, and forcefulness can be, to some degree, imitated. A writer—speech writer, journalist, novelist, or poet—has personal insights, convictions, bias, prejudice, experience, understanding, and awareness. These elements are unique to each individual. These elements cannot be imitated. And these elements are the essential and incommunicable foundation of style.

A speech is supposed to reflect the writer. A speech should get its soul, its breath of life, from the author.

There are a number of useful "do's and don'ts" that should prove helpful in developing a style for speech writing. For the novice speech writer, I suggest that these guides be applied when he reviews the first speech draft. After a few speeches have been written, perhaps even by the time the first speech is ready for delivery, certain techniques will become tools of style.

DO—AVOID THE USE OF THE PASSIVE VOICE AT EVERY OPPORTUNITY

In the last two decades the use of the passive voice has become widespread, especially in various writings from the technically oriented industries such as electronics, physics, chemistry, and in administrative and support functions allied with those disciplines. In writing a speech, the technically oriented professional man will find that he relies heavily on the passive voice.

The passive voice shows that the subject is acted upon by another. It is mildly ironic to note that passive voice can only be defined accurately by using the passive voice. The word "passive" comes from a Latin verb meaning "to suffer." The subject suffers, the action suffers, the sentence suffers—and the audience suffers.

The passive voice is necessary; it is also artificial. To say, "It is suggested by the author" in place of "I suggest" or "The author suggests" is to completely negate the force of language. To write a speech filled with passive-voice verbs is to increase volume alone by about 100 to 300 per cent in verb forms.

Speeches filled with "It has been pointed out by," "It is understood by all," "It has been said by," and "It is to be noted that" drain the life out of the speech. The passive voice robs the writing of force, pep, punch—the passive voice certainly makes the writing inactive, literally and figuratively.

DO—USE THE FIRST PERSON PRONOUN

It is a false modesty that says, "The speaker should avoid the use of the first person pronoun." The audience wants to hear your thoughts, your convictions, your opinions on the speech topic. The speaker can and should say "I think," "I believe," "I understand," and "It's my opinion, though only an opinion". The audience expects you to stand behind your remarks.

DON'T—USE THE SO-CALLED "EDITORIAL WE"

The first person plural is sometimes called the "plural of majesty." The expression has lived many centuries; it is still used by heads of state such as the President of the United States, the Roman Catholic Pope, and others. If the statement in a speech refers to the "actual we"—the members of some association—then the use is correct.

DO—TRY TO STYLIZE THE PROSE ENDINGS OF SENTENCES

This is an advanced technique in writing but a method worth developing in speech writing. The beginning and end of a sentence are the points of emphasis. The concluding words in a sentence are usually delivered with less volume to "let the sentence down" from its opening vocal level. Clumsy, harsh word order at the end of the sentence is unpleasing to hear. The sentence should glide toward an ending, not be dropped.

A few examples here will clarify the concept. The sentence ending with the words "maligning each day" would both read and sound more pleasing if written "daily maligning." The second ending is let down gently; the first example ends in two abrupt monosyllables.

To avoid confusing the reader I state again that the most effective writing for a speech is lean, tight writing. The rhythmic prose endings *may* be useful for two or three important ideas in a speech, where a particular thought is to be emphasized and a greater impression made on the audience. There are other, more common figures of speech which can help improve the style of writing; the Appendix contains explanations and examples of these literary devices.

DO—ALLOW SOME SPONTANEOUS GENERATION OF THE "TURN OF PHRASE"

This expression means the unique grouping of words in a particularly forceful way. The "turn of phrase" is the writer's insight into a concept; it is, in the genuine sense, a clever way, a novel way of expressing an idea; it is a new way of looking at things. The spontaneity of the "turn of phrase" is a loose way of defining how the right words seem to drop into place. Much thought, conscious or preconscious, precedes the final-choice phrase. There is no formula for writing the "happy" phrase; the right combination is intuitively grasped.

DO—TRY TO MAKE FREQUENT USE OF THE TRIAD

The triad is simply a "grouping of threes"—words, phrases, clauses, even sentences—to achieve a dramatic effect. For some mysterious reason, and that is no cliché, the series of three has been part of man's communication attempts since at least the time of Greek literature. Western culture has been generally fascinated by the triad; we are still fascinated today. The use of the triad is an extremely effective device for the speech writer. The triad imparts force to the writer's concepts; the triad makes the listener take note; the triad insures development of thought—and the remembrance of it.

The effectiveness of the triad can be judged by a random sampling of examples from literature:

"Never in the field of human conflict was *so much* owed by *so many* to *so few*."

> Winston S. Churchill
> *Tribute to the Royal Air Force*
> House of Commons, August 20, 1940

". . . we cannot dedicate—we cannot consecrate—we cannot hallow—this ground."

> Abraham Lincoln
> *Address at Gettysburg*
> November 10, 1893

"For thine is the kingdom, the power, and the glory."

> *The Lord's Prayer*

"Friends, Romans, countrymen; lend me your ears."

> William Shakespeare
> *Julius Caesar*

"Hit hard, hit fast, hit often."

> Admiral William F. Halsey
> *Formula for Waging War*

It is well worth the effort to develop this element of style. And it is fairly easy to develop this technique if the speech writer does not strain after the triad.

If the implications of the speech topic are given some thought, the speech writer will find that the major points of the outline develop quite easily. The same is true when those major points are evaluated for their latent content. The "triadic" influence is felt not only in sentence composition but also in the entire speech structure.

Most events do not occur in isolation; they have effects on the respective environment. A new piece of legislation may have social, legal, moral, and financial implications. A company idled by strike affects customers, vendors, and a community. Automation affects costs, production, and workers.

DO—VARY THE PACE OF WRITING

A speech that uses the same style patterns paragraph after paragraph, and sentence after sentence, will soon hypnotize the audience. The hypnosis may cause the audience to assume a "paying-attention" posture, but they frequently will hear sounds and not words; words but not ideas; and sentences without relation. A monotonous style is as devastating as a monotonous tone.

To help vary the pace of the writing, the speech writer can use the following ideas where applicable. Shorten sentences. Lengthen sentences. Use a telegraphic style. Ask questions in the text. Avoid complicated sentences. Make topic sentences forceful. Use figures of speech. Try pleasant-sounding words. Try harsh-sounding words. Slip in some poetic meter, occasionally.

Other techniques will suggest themselves to the writer as he visually and orally reviews the speech draft. Incidentally, remember that the speeches that impressed you—the "good" ones—just didn't happen. Certainly, the speaker had something worthwhile to say; *how* he said it caused the impression on you. This is why style—your style—is so important to the speech.

SUMMARY CHECK LIST

Avoid passive voice
Use the first person pronoun
Write spontaneously
Use triads
Vary the pace of writing

11

ALMOST READY TO WRITE

When an outline has been written, and the research material has been compiled and evaluated, it is time to think about writing. The neophyte speech writer may ask, "How do I start writing?" The answer is clear and direct: "Start writing." Several specific guides to help the writer compose his speech are explained in detail. There are a few preliminaries before writing.

LENGTH OF A SPEECH

How long should a speech be? There is no hard and fast rule, no absolute standard for time limits. Professional speech writers generally agree, however, that a 20-minute speech is plenty of time to speak. The blunt argument supporting this opinion states, "If you can't make your point in twenty minutes of talking, no additional time will help you do it."

Also the writer should try to think of the audience. Courtesy expressed in brevity can win many an audience. Additionally, the less material the audience hears, the greater the possibility it will remember and retain the speaker's key remarks.

Psychologists concerned with the mental processes have established that about 70 percent of spoken material is forgotten one hour after it is heard. Someone has summarized this question of speech length very nicely by saying, "The more you tell them, the more they will forget."

This same memory-retention process demands that a speech be forceful, plain, direct, and uncluttered in both language and structure. The process also requires that repetition be an integral element of the written speech. If "repetition is the mother of learning," skillful repetition is the mother of good speech writing.

TIME REQUIRED FOR WRITING

Based upon a speech time limit of 20 minutes, the writer should estimate that he needs a minimum of one hour for each final, ready-to-deliver minute of the speech. The time may increase to two hours for each minute, depending on the speech topic. The time required for writing is a composite of time needed for all nonwriting factors, such as research, outline of speech, review, criticism, and approval. The hour-per-minute rule of thumb does not include extensive rewriting of the speech. That feature of speech writing is played strictly by ear.

On the average, a speaker will use about 2.5 minutes to deliver one typewritten page of the text. Increasing or trimming the length of the speech will obviously require time. Ordinarily, the speech can be easily and legitimately increased by getting additional material from the research sources. Frankly, a well-written speech is sometimes deliberately lengthened to meet both the 20-minute standard or an authoritative request for a lengthier speech.

Trimming the speech is not time consuming. This chore is comparatively easy for the writer; paragraphs and entire pages can be deleted. With a careful rewriting of the text surrounding the deleted portions, the speech will suffer no substantial damage.

VARIABLES AFFECTING TIME SCHEDULE

The variables contained in the speech theme are less tangible elements, and their influence on "time needed to write" is difficult to measure. To help the speech writer understand the importance of these variables, I have listed a number of factors that affect the writer's timetable. The speech writer alone can evaluate those factors.

1. Familiarity with the subject matter of the speech topic.
2. Availability of research sources.
3. The writer's facility with language.
4. Previous experience in writing.

5. Previous speech-writing efforts.

6. Type of audience.

7. Writer's ideas, feelings, prejudice, and bias toward the speech topic.

One final suggestion before you start your speech. When the speech outline is finished, and when all the research sources have been marked, clipped, reedited and reorganized, take five or ten minutes to condition your writing faculties.

The speech writer might try to create an environment for the speech. Often the context he defines can help establish the level and the tone of his speech. The writer can easily observe that in the course of writing, his skill, intellect, and imagination progressively function more effectively, productively, and smoothly. If he will create the setting for the speech before he starts to write, he will find that the opening sections of the text come quite close to the level and tone of the inner portions of the speech.

SUMMARY CHECK LIST

Write a 20-minute speech
Use skillful repetition
Create environment for the speech
Typed page: 2.5 minutes of speaking time

12

AS YOU WRITE

At this point, start the work of writing your speech. In writing the first draft of a speech, or the first draft of a first speech, the observance of certain "axioms" will help insure maximum return on your time and effort. These axioms are (1) write out the speech, (2) follow the outline, (3) think paragraphs, (4) assume nothing, and (5) avoid the periodic sentence.

AXIOM I: WRITE OUT THE SPEECH

This axiom means, "Write out the speech in full." Do just that; write down every word of it. The novice speech writer should never even consider *not* writing out his speech.

A speech must have definite physical limits: subject matter, time, style, research facts, opinions, arguments—in short, all the elements of a speech have boundaries. To ensure that all of these elements receive proper definition they must be contained, locked in, pinned down. Writing is the only dependable method of doing this. It is virtually impossible to prepare an original, well-written speech in the abstract. Writing a speech is a difficult assignment even when the thoughts are captured on paper.

Besides, educational psychologists offer strong evidence that the mind's concentration on a single concept does not exceed 30 seconds. Under this limitation, the preparation of a speech in the abstract would be an exercise in mental gymnastics: intellectually intriguing but, practically, fruitless.

The speech writer certainly can bear witness to the uncanny flightiness of thought. How often has a conversation, or shooting the breeze, or a business meeting started with one topic, covered many unrelated subjects, and wound up far-removed from the original idea?

Let us experiment. Choose any idea you wish. Check the time on your watch, and make a strong effort to concentrate on that chosen idea, and that idea alone. When you become aware that your thinking is not on the topic, check your watch again. Determine how long you have been thinking and the number of topics that went through your mind. Writing out the speech confines thought, directs thought, and stimulates thought.

The speech writer is urged to adopt this axiom: write out the speech in full.

AXIOM II: FOLLOW THE OUTLINE

Follow the outline without deviation until the first draft of the speech is written. Follow the outline, but do not be inflexible in expressing your thoughts under each point of the outline. If new ideas, different aspects of old ideas, fresh insights, a quotation, or comparisons come to mind—no matter what flowing and spontaneous thoughts on the speech occur—write them down when they occur. Do not shut off the stream of thought. The speech writer can always reject ideas when he reviews the draft. Perhaps the outline will need revision, but that can be done after writing the speech.

Write out your speech, point by point, just as the outline indicates.

AXIOM III: THINK PARAGRAPHS

One dictionary defines a paragraph as "a distinct portion of written matter dealing with a particular idea." That dry-as-dust definition is likely to stop the speech writer in his tracks. There is one consideration about the paragraph, however, that is worth noting.

The paragraph is the *sine qua non* of speech writing.

If the writer cannot fashion paragraphs, he had better learn before he attempts speech writing.

Also, that particularly bland and abstract definition of a paragraph contains the phrase "with a particular idea." That "idea" is the topic sentence. If the paragraph is absolutely indispensable to speech writing, the topic sentence is the reason for making that statement.

The topic sentence determines paragraph structure and thought continuity.

The most common defect in speeches written today is the failure to establish a connection between paragraphs. Continuity of thought is either overlooked or ignored. As a result, the speech is difficult to follow, hard to understand, and easy to forget.

A writer figuratively builds a speech. The paragraph is the building block. Thought continuity is the cement that joins the blocks into a unified structure. At the risk of overstating the case for the paragraph I suggest that the writer constantly remind himself that he must move from point A to point B in the speech. He must continually make a clear, obvious, and logical transition from one paragraph to the next.

The reason for emphasizing transition is that the novice speech writer has a blind spot in putting his thoughts in writing. Because of his research on the subject matter of the speech, he enjoys a familiar knowledge on the topic. His outline gives him directions for writing, but his mind plays tricks on him by suppressing some of the processes that lead to conclusion; and because he has prepared well he will make judgments without realizing that a connecting bond is missing. The pivotal thought, which is the nexus of the argument, is suppressed so that the conclusion can be quickly reached. It is the nature of the reasoning process, according to one school of thought, and it is necessary to avoid making all conclusions depend upon a formal syllogism.

AXIOM IV: "ASSUME NOTHING"

Write your speech as if your audience had never heard of the topic. This just might be the case. The speech writer must make every special term clear. He must explain every novel approach. He must define, qualify, illustrate, and support every conclusion that he draws.

An example will show one way to employ the axiom.

In the following hypothetical situation a speaker is giving a talk titled "Unemployment in the Future" at a Junior Chamber of Commerce luncheon.

The speech is based on the educated opinion that automation will reduce economic problems. In the speech the statement is made that "By 1984, I am convinced that automation will have practically eliminated unemployment."

The statement is attention getting. At the same time, many of the listeners will interpret the speaker's remark quite differently from its intended meaning. His statement will also raise a number of questions.

If the writer is inattentive to his statement, he will let the remark stand, without any attempt to define the meaning. Most probably, he will launch into a description of the techniques of automation, and continue on with the rest of the speech.

The thoughtful speech writer will justify the statement and anticipate the questions regarding it. He will limit the misinterpretation of his remarks by a clear, precise, and direct definition of his terms. He will provide answers.

To continue with the example, "automation" is the technique, method, or system of operating or controlling a mechanical or productive process by highly automatic means. By definition, then, the speaker is limiting his remark to mechanical and production operations. He is talking essentially about factory workers. But the audience will not know those restrictions unless he informs them.

Certainly, the word "automation" is in common usage; however, the speech writer cannot assume that his entire audience knows precisely what the term means. It really does not matter whether the audience has some knowledge of the subject; the writer must define *his* thoughts precisely.

The writer might define the term, or his use of the term, along these lines: "Automation, as you may know (or "It is generally agreed that automation means. . . ."), is the automatic operation of mechanical and production processes. It is, of course, limited to the factory, and the factory worker."

By this qualifying and explanatory comment the writer has set the limits to his statement. He is not writing about office workers, sales people, service businesses, and the like, he is writing about the factory worker, and how unemployment in this class will be reduced by automation.

To his audience the word "unemployment" has many modes. To

the writer "unemployment" is used in a restricted sense. In his speech it does not mean anyone who is not working, but he must tell the audience how he is using the term.

He might handle that term in this way: "The U.S. Bureau of Labor Statistics defines an unemployed person as 'one who is both out of a job and actively seeking employment.' "

This explanation makes considerable difference to the audience. Unemployment does not strictly apply to the housewife who worked just to get out of the house, but has now willingly returned to homemaking. Unemployment does not apply to the college boy who earned tuition money in a summer factory job, but has now returned to campus. He is not working, to be sure, but he cannot count in unemployment statistics.

The well-constructed explanation of the topic sentence on "unemployment" may be written as follows:

"I am convinced that automation will have practically eliminated unemployment by 1984."

"Automation, as you may know, is the automatic operation of production and manufacturing processes. The word automation affects both factory and factory workers."

"Automation will reduce unemployment. The Bureau of Labor Statistics defines an unemployed person as 'one who is out of work and actively seeking employment.' Unemployment does not apply to the housewife who takes a temporary job for 'fast, fast, fast relief' from housework and kids. Unemployment does not apply to the college student who took a summer job, but is now back on campus. Certainly, both persons are out of work. But strictly speaking, they are not 'unemployed.' "

Then the writer can move forward to the other sections of the speech.

The axiom "assume nothing" urges the writer to define his terms.

AXIOM V: AVOID PERIODIC SENTENCES

It is almost a truism to state that English literature owes much to the ancient Latin and Greek writers. Their elegance of style, command of language, and journalistic craftsmanship so captivated Western civilization that these writers were judged models of excellence for all writers.

And yet I suggest we return that one model of excellence called the "periodic sentence" to classical antiquity. An analysis of the device will show why.

The periodic sentence can be defined as follows:

"That sentence in which a number of clauses, dependent on a principle clause, are so elaborately and stylishly arranged that the action of the main clause is not expressed until the end of the sentence to produce an effect of suspense." (I add: "or confusion, or frustration, or unintelligence.")

The definition is almost as involved as the example that follows. This "model" periodic sentence is fashioned after Cicero, the exemplar of such writing:

"Is it within the province of this august senate, where men of such learning and nobility reside, who steeped in legislative experience and skill and well knowing indeed that morals, laws and good order are affected by their conduct, to attempt a cruel and senseless revision of a charter which has been purchased by the blood, sweat, and tears of patriots?"

The reader will get a true appreciation of the periodic sentence by removing all punctuation from the example and rearranging the clauses as he pleases.

Latin word order in a sentence is much more fluid than English word order; also, the Latins were quite frugal with punctuation. The model sentence above is a fairly close imitation of the Latin periodic style.

In reading a periodic sentence, there is at least a chance to understand the thought, because the sentence can be re-read repeatedly, until a reasonably clear meaning is extracted.

An audience will find it virtually impossible to comprehend a speech that is full of periodic sentences.

First, all sentence components must be *remembered*, with judgment suspended, until the main thought is reached at the end. This is asking too much of the listener. Moreover, the speaker will continue talking while the audience is grappling with the periodic sentence; subsequent statements will be missed.

The writing of periodic sentences is an unhappy talent of the educated and professionally oriented person. I have experienced sentences twice as long as the example shown earlier. The periodic sentence may have merit as prose composition, but it is poor, poor speechifying.

One of the speech writer's tasks is to make sentences manageable units of thought. If the writer usually composes in the periodic style, he should reject that method and train himself to write easily handled sentences. Careful analysis of a periodic sentence will show that there are a number of smaller sentences latent in the subordinate clauses. If the reduction of a periodic sentence proves especially difficult, the speech writer might ask someone to read the sentence and to list every group of words that seem to be independent units of thought.

The best remedy for this style of writing is: avoid periodic sentences.

SUMMARY CHECK LIST

Write out the speech
Follow the outline
Think paragraphs
Assume nothing
Avoid periodic sentences

13
CRITICISM

Criticism is a harsh-sounding word. Criticism also seems to have a harsh connotation, so we generally avoid the word. We ask someone to "review," "comment," "evaluate," and "suggest." It is the rare speech writer who says, "Please criticize this speech I have written."

Criticism of a speech is absolutely necessary. The speech writer should be critical of his own writing; he should also seek criticism of each finished draft. Through criticism, the writer can produce a good speech, and can continue developing and refining the techniques of good speech writing. No speech writer worth his salt will issue a speech for delivery without getting a critical appraisal of it before its release.

If there is one definitive statement to be made in this book, it is found here: "Always, without exception, and under *every* circumstance, have another person criticize your speech draft." To issue the speech upon your approval alone is tantamount to professional suicide, whether the writer is a scientist, engineer, businessman, or (even worse) a speech writer.

Such criticism rarely descends to the personal level. Therefore the speech writer should rarely consider criticism as a personal attack. The speech writer who is bothered by criticism might well consider not writing anymore.

THE WRITER CRITICIZES

It is only fair that the writer of the speech should make the first critical review. But he should never begin his review five minutes after the first draft is finished. The minimum cooling-off period should be over-night, if possible. If the speech draft can be set aside for a few days, so much the better. In any case, the writer can review the speech crit-ically if he has not been enmeshed in it for a while.

The writer should judge each sentence and each paragraph on its merits; he should evaluate these elements: leanness, clarity, contin-uity, grammar, and style.

The speech writer should make the changes as needed. If rewriting is necessary, rewrite. If deletion is called for, delete. Trim whenever "tight writing" will be the result.

CRITICISM BY OTHERS

Criticism by another offers both an objective appraisal of your speech writing and the reaction of a person who could be considered as an "audience." The critic's reaction to the speech is a clue to the reaction of the future audience.

Don't ask a good friend or a subordinate to criticize the speech for you. The reasons for that statement are simple enough: the friend will tell you what you want to hear; the subordinate won't tell you what you should hear.

Ask some qualified but noninvolved person to review the speech. Tell him to look for the same things you look for in criticizing the draft. And tell him that other criticisms will also be appreciated.

Don't be anxious about the criticism. There is some physiological reaction when the critic returns your manuscript and you wonder "How bad is it?"

If the speech critic has done his work well, he will find a few minor, though not unimportant, mistakes, and he will point out a few notable lapses. Generally, this is all you will get in criticism. One or two sin-cere suggestions may be offered, and the whole dread episode will be finished.

The contributions of the critic, handled with a light touch, are not to be minimized. These "few notable lapses" that he points out might mean good speech or poor speech, so give proper attention to his com-ments.

14

THE WRITER AS SPEAKER

It is an understatement to say that this chapter is not a treatise on public speaking. Instead, it is a brief treatment of some speaking problems that affect the delivery of a speech. Here, we are basically concerned with the *sound* of the speech and the man who makes those sounds, the speaker. In the next chapter some techniques of speech rehearsal are discussed.

HOW DO YOU SOUND TO OTHERS?

To make improvements in speaking, the speaker needs a point of reference, a place to begin. That starting point is with yourself. How do you sound to others? What do you think you sound like? There is a quick, nonscientific, and fairly accurate method to find out.

Simply cup your hands behind your ears and push the ears slightly forward. Then speak. Surprised? That's how you sound to others. Don't walk around the office that way; but do make some use of this help in practicing the speech.

Many defects are the results of nervousness. If the speaker sounds like Jerry Lewis all the time, the voice techniques covered here will not benefit him. The purpose here is to free the speaker of the impediments that arise from just plain nervousness. This understandable and necessary nervousness affects speed of delivery, pitch of voice, and breathing. It will also affect your speech patterns.

SPEED OF DELIVERY

The inexperienced speaker usually speaks about twice as fast as he thinks he speaks. At least twice as fast. Delivering a speech is an uncomfortable chore for many people and, to resolve the situation as fast as possible, they speed up the rate of delivery. High speed makes it difficult for the audience to grasp your words; without a grasp of the words, they can't know what you mean. Frequently, the audience is irritated and, occasionally, someone in the audience will ask you to slow down.

Slowing yourself down requires conscious, continuous effort. Here are some ways to attempt this. Remind yourself, as you speak, to slow down. Make a deliberate pause between each sentence. Speak your words with precision; don't slur them. The speaker is cautioned not to exaggerate any of these items. An audience will also react if the speaker is too slow. So, the speed of delivery is established by trial and error and by constant practice, until you, perhaps with help, arrive at an acceptable rate.

PITCH OF VOICE

Nervousness tightens up the vocal cords. When someone tries to speak with this physical restriction, squeaky tones and "cracked" sounds result. Nervousness also restricts breathing. Generally, as the speaker progresses into the speech, the tight nervousness leaves him; his voice returns to normal pitch. This particular phenomenon is well-documented by public speakers.

BREATHING DIFFICULTY

The big hurdle for the speaker occurs in the first few paragraphs of the speech. Once he gets past them, he will be more at ease. It has been found in one study that the solar plexus is the control center for the diaphragm. When the solar plexus is affected by nervousness, the diaphragm is restricted, and breathing becomes difficult. That "pit-of-the-stomach" feeling of nervousness comes close to describing the actual area causing the discomfort.

One way to relax the solar plexus is to breathe deeply, hold your breath for a few seconds, then exhale as fully as possible. Do this three times, and you will eliminate much of the breathing tightness. Remember: do this exercise discreetly; on the way to the speaker's stand, or at the table, or off stage. Don't let the audience see you warming up; they may misread you.

SPEECH PATTERNS

The way we speak is habitual with us, unless public speaking courses changed the patterns. We all speak in a pattern peculiar to us. Since these patterns are part of us, and have been for some time, we are generally not aware of them. We are not conscious of our clipped and abrupt sounds, or our sing-song delivery, or a deadly monotone, or how many times we say "Uh . . . Uh" as we speak. Also, there are certain words that are difficult, if not impossible, for us to pronounce correctly.

The use of the tape recorder is highly recommended for evaluating and correcting speech patterns.

THE TAPE RECORDER

When recording the speech, read directly from the first draft. Read the speech exactly as you think you will deliver it before an audience.

On the playback listen to the voice as if it were the voice of a stranger. Bring critical awareness to the listening. At first, limit your listening to about one quarter of the speech; for a 20-minute speech, listen to five minutes of it. Repeat this three or four times. Peculiarities of your speaking should show up. Make a note of each specific pattern—sing-song, "Uh . . . Uh," and the like.

Once the patterns have been spotted, take the speech draft and read it as you listen to the entire taped speech. Make notes on the draft where changes are to be made. When retyping the draft, type cues in the text in capitals, in parentheses. Cues such as (FORCE), (SLOW), (PAUSE), and (LOOK UP) can be quite helpful to the speaker.

SOUND LEVEL

The availability of the microphone has eliminated one of the toughest parts of speaking: trying to be heard by a large audience. If a "mike" is unavailable for speaking, mark the places in the text where you will need a pause for breathing. Two diagonal lines (//) can indicate a breathing spot.

SUMMARY CHECK LIST

Speak slowly
Relax to breathe easier
Check voice patterns
Use "cues" in speech

15

THE WRITER REHEARSES: SOME GUIDES

The saying "practice makes perfect" is, at best, a half-truth; only *perfect* practice makes perfect. Much effort can be saved if the speaker will observe that corrected maxim. As you rehearse your speech, don't waste time and effort constantly repeating portions that you have already mastered. Spend your time perfecting the awkward points in the talk.

There are idiosyncrasies common to every delivery of a speech. The experienced speaker keeps these to a minimum, or makes them work in his behalf. The delivery defects most likely to be noticed by an audience, which is then distracted from the speech, are described below.

It is important to remedy these delivery defects. The words we speak are only one form of communication; the gestures, idiosyncrasies, and peculiarities we display before an audience also communicate. "They" should say what the speaker says.

ROCK AND ROLL

The era of "rock and roll" is over for the teenagers, but the rhythm lives on in many speakers. Relax. Stand straight. Don't rock back and forth; if anything, lean into the audience. Don't roll from side to side, it looks like the audience is watching tennis as it tries to follow your motions.

STARING INTO SPACE

Many speakers are unable to look at the audience. No contact, no bond; no bond, no impression. Look at the people in the audience. Look them all over, speak to different sections of the audience as you give your speech. The audience is watching you, so you better watch them. They know that you are not looking at them when your eyes are aiming 45° above the horizon. Look down, into their faces, and establish a bond with them.

GESTURES

Use them. Let them be spontaneous. Let them give physical force to your words. Using gestures is not "acting," and there is no reason to be self-conscious about them. It is a rare conversation, rather a dead conversation, where the speakers do not gesticulate. Watch all the people the next time you join in "shooting the breeze."

Use your hands, your eyebrows, your shoulders, where they naturally dramatize your point. Use your fist, hand, index finger; enumerate one, two, three with your fingers when the text calls for it. Tug on your ear at some knotty statement or question in the speech.

Let the gestures be spontaneous, yes. Let them be used judiciously, when a sentence seems to call for a gesture.

REHEARSING THE SPEECH

Keep rehearsing until you're sure you have the speech down "cold." Practice out loud, in an empty office, the cellar, or the attic. But practice out loud. It is assumed that the speaker practices "on his feet."

When you think the speech is exactly the way you want it, deliver it nonstop. When you make a mistake, keep on speaking. The delivery before a live audience will probably have some stumbling point in it; a cough, a sneeze, a sudden noise can throw you off balance, so don't be concerned about a mistake in delivery. Still, try for perfect practice. At the very least you'll minimize the risk of stumbling.

Don't think that constant practice will rob the speech of vitality. The rehearsal and the real thing are far different situations. There will be enough nervousness and increased adrenalin to give you a new experience in speaking before your audience.

Time your speech. See if it comes near the time set by you or others. If your time comes within three minutes, either way, don't change the speech. Most probably you were asked to give a speech "around" so many minutes long.

One comment to conclude this chapter and prepare for the next: The man who wants to be a good speaker does not read his speech to the audience, nor does he memorize the speech. . . .

SUMMARY CHECK LIST

Practice perfectly
Look at the audience
Stay in one place
Use gestures
Time your speech

16

MEMORIZING A SPEECH

There are three guidelines on this subject:

1. Do not memorize.
2. Do not try to memorize.
3. Do not even consider memorizing.

These three statements are direct, strong, and uncompromising. Some reasons for the three negatives are given below. As a rule, the memorized speech affects both the speaker and the audience.

EFFECTS ON THE SPEAKER

The speaker is at the mercy of his memory when he decides to deliver a memorized speech. *Every* speaker who memorizes a speech is saddled with that liability. The speaker knows that memory is tricky; it may desert him at any moment. Memory is such a fickle faculty; the slightest distraction can cause it to go blank. When this happens, the speaker is left without a word of the speech in his head.

Simple and quite common audience happenings such as a cough, a sneeze, or a door slamming can shut off the recall process. Audience noise levels are high; there is a good deal of collateral activity going on, even in the quietest group. People rustle programs; they shift, they squirm, and they do impolite and uncouth things. The hearing and the seeing of audience activities can cause the speaker to focus on any one of those actions, much to the detriment of his memory.

Memorizing the speech demands an enormous amount of time and energy for most people. Frankly, a small percentage of speakers do have marvelous memories. They can memorize a speech in a couple of readings. Most of us do not have this ability. Memorizing by rote is tedious, time consuming, and tenuous.

EFFECTS ON THE AUDIENCE

An audience can generally detect a memorized speech. For some reason, an audience reacts adversely to the speech when it is delivered from memory, at least in my experience. One possible explanation is that the speaker is not establishing a bond with his audience; he is not getting involved with them. Really, the speaker of the memorized speech is primarily concerned with recalling that speech. The speaker is not the master of the moment; he must figuratively stand aside and let memory do the work for him. The speaker's audience is of only secondary concern to him. It seems that the audience, even in a vague way, senses that the action never gets beyond the microphone.

DON'T MEMORIZE.

17

THE INDEX CARD AND YOU

Previously it was stated: "The good speaker does not read his speech to the audience." Also the speaker was strongly urged not to memorize his speech.

The logical question then arises: "What does the speaker use as a speech vehicle?" Index cards are recommended; the 5 × 7 inch card, not the 3 × 5 inch card. The larger card can hold more typewritten material, which is easier to read than handwritten notes. The smaller index card will not hold much typed or written material.

Any inconvenience in using the 5 × 7 inch cards will be trifling compared to the benefits to be gained.

ON THE CARDS

The cards should contain the speech components listed below.

1. *Title of Speech.* With preliminary remarks, names of individuals and groups pertinent to the occasion.

2. *Outline.* One card for each major section of the outline, with detailed subheadings under each section, plus material below, where applicable.

3. *Quotations.* Especially those that have involved structure or depend on word play for effect.

4. *Key Examples.* Exact dates, statistics, names, and attribution should be listed.

5. *Key Phrases.* Personal turns of phrase, ideas that demand repetition, difficult words syllabicated for pronunciation, and the like.

6. *Cues.* For delivery techniques: SLOW, FAST, PAUSE, LOOK AT AUDIENCE, GESTURES, and RAISE VOICE.

REHEARSING WITH CARDS

Once the speech is well in hand in rehearsal, the speaker should continue rehearsing with the use of the index cards.

The speech rehearsal should be so thorough that the cards serve as "prompters." If the rehearsal has been one of perfect practice, the speaker will feel at ease and confident after a few tries with these cards. Incidentally, the speech outline should be typed on the *unlined* side of the index card. The lined side can be an annoying distraction reading your notes.

AT SPEECH TIME

Take the index cards, and the cards only, to the speaker's place. If you brought the speech manuscript with you, leave it somewhere. Use just the cards at the microphone. If you have time before delivering the speech, check the speaker's area for microphone controls, lights, loose wiring on the floor, and a place to put your cards.

If you are requested to shorten the speech, simply cross out some of the minor subheads in sections; you know how long your delivery time is, if you have rehearsed with the cards. If you ever get a request to lengthen the speech before you go on, ignore it. The host is responsible for finding fill-in time.

One final word: the index-card technique is practiced by many speakers. It is an excellent technique for the novice speaker. It helps the speaker to talk to his audience—to communicate with them instead of talk at them. The technique helps present you as you really are in a conversation: animated and saying something, but relaxed and confident. And the audience will get this impression.

SUMMARY CHECK LIST

Index Card Outline of Speech

4. THE PROBLEM NOW

—*Senator Jones:* In serious political trouble; he is a "dove"; constituents
    are "hawks." Chance to get back popularity by attacking taxes.

—*Cosgrove's Book:*
        —advertising versus R&D; 4x for ads as R&D
        —ignores contributions of auto makers (GNP & standard of
        living)
    * —slanted, selective, sensational versions of mistakes
        —cf. *Chicago Tribune* and *Miami Herald* feature stories.

—*Public Opinion:*
        —against manufacturers of hardware: $$ additional
        —"bad press" making sensationalism
        —information must come from mfrs.; full program needed.

18

MOMENT OF TRUTH: YOU SPEAK

The first few minutes of speaking are the toughest test for both experienced and occasional speakers. Although this chapter is directed to the occasional speaker, it may have some value for the regular speaker, who still is bothered by nervousness.

Nervousness, stage fright, butterflies—call it what you will—it is the one essential and inescapable element of every speech. Nervousness is normal, necessary and, in a certain sense, commendable. In my opinion, you will not make a good speech unless you are nervous.

If you fear speaking before an audience, relax; you have membership in a huge club with noteworthy members such as Cicero, the Roman orator and writer, and Churchill, statesman, speaker, and author. Cicero confesses that he was always nervous when he started giving a speech. We know for a fact that in one instance, a trial, Cicero was so afraid that he botched his speech, left the courtroom, and lost his case.

Churchill's contemporaries tell us that he cared little for speeches, and had great distaste for broadcasting his speeches. It is reported also that he took a while getting his speaking skills functioning whenever he gave a speech to Parliament.

GOOD FEATURES OF NERVOUSNESS

What in heaven's name, you ask, can be "good" about nervousness? For a starter, you can assume nervousness means that you do care about what you are going to say to an audience. If you really didn't care about doing a good job as a speaker, you wouldn't be nervous.

Second, being nervous puts you above your ordinary, routine way of doing things. Nervousness is a stimulant to the speaker, if he controls it. This stimulant can put you above your natural level and talent. Instead of stage fright, convert the energy into enthusiasm, vigor, and dynamic—but natural—gestures.

Besides, if you have prepared well, the nervousness will be reduced automatically as you proceed in your delivery. About one third or halfway through your talk, you will usually become conscious of the fact that you are no longer "scared." You still really are, but not to the degree that you experienced at the start of the speech. You have things under confident control now, and if you think you are putting the message across, you feel like you could talk much longer.

IF YOU MUFF YOUR LINES

Suppose you do flub a sentence or some words or get lost in the speech? What do you do? For one thing don't run off the stage. Stop where you are. Go back to the last-remembered thought in the outline, get your bearings, and before you start simply excuse the flub by saying to the audience: "I seem to have missed a turn in the road somewhere," or, "One fellow who used to do this regularly got to be President of the United States" (JFK).

AUDIENCE REACTION

An audience certainly knows when a speaker is extremely nervous. And they obviously know when you make a mistake in speaking.

But the audience is on your side. Some of them were, some are, some will, and some will continue to be speechmakers, and they know only too well how a speaker can become derailed in a speech. You, as a speaker, enjoy the sympathy of the audience; they're pulling for you.

If you have prepared your speech well, if you honestly have something to say, if you obviously have spent time on the speech—and this is easy to spot—the audience will give you a fair hearing. They won't boo, they won't hiss, and they won't start throwing things.

CAUSES OF NERVOUSNESS

Reading a book by a psychologist would be the only way to get a detailed, clinical answer to the problem of nervousness.

But I believe that a major factor behind "speaker's jitters" is preoccupation with one's self. We analyze, talk and think ourselves into the state of extreme nervousness. Am I prepared? Suppose I. . . . What if they. . . . Did I. . . . How about. . . . We worry ourselves about ourselves.

After all, we are not being asked to stand up and deliver the Toreador song from Carmen. As speakers, we are still using the thing that we are most familiar with—language; we are still among the creatures most familiar to us—humans; and we are only asked to do what we have been doing all our lives—communicate. To be concerned about our speaking is commendable; to be tormented about it saps our energy and talent.

SOME STEPS TO CONTROL STAGE FRIGHT

Only general rules can be offered here; the problem is personal and demands a personal solution. Assuming that the speechmaker has prepared extremely well, he might then condition himself to forget three things on the day of delivery:

1. Forget about yourself.
2. Forget about the speech.
3. Forget about the audience.

Chapter 14, "The Writer as Speaker," contains some helpful hints on overcoming, or at least restricting, the major speaking defects caused by nervousness.

19

REACHING OTHER AUDIENCES

"Take a newspaper some day and see how much of the news in it is not about what someone *did,* but rather about what someone *said.*" (The italics are mine.)

This remark of R. C. Alberts, a public relations vice president of Ketchum, MacLeod & Grove, appeared in a recent issue of the *Public Relations Journal.* His statement is the foundation for this chapter.

THE SECOND AND THIRD AUDIENCES

The group that listens to the speech is only "Audience One." Two other audiences can be reached by the speech: the national business community and the governmental communities (federal, state, and local). The speechmaker delivers his remarks to an audience ranging from hundreds to perhaps a few thousand listeners. Through the printed version of his speech, he can reach millions of people nation-wide.

His aims are to initiate a policy, to help establish a new approach, or to be a spokesman for a segment of the people and state a position —these are the broad and compelling reasons for making a speech— and seeing that it is carried in print.

ADVANCE COPIES AND WHERE TO PLACE THEM

The speechmaker should decide how many copies of the speech should be printed for advance distribution. Ordinarily the group hosting the speaker will ask for copies to distribute among the communications media in the speaking locale. This will ensure local coverage; the speaker should also have additional copies of the speech available for handouts to the audience and to any press people present.

In addition, copies of the speech, with the release date clearly noted on the first page, should be mailed in advance to the business and financial editors of the country's leading newspapers and national magazines. A brief note of explanation should accompany the speech. Ideally, the time to get the speech in other hands is before the speaking date.

To ensure a better chance for national coverage (depending on the subject), the speech should be on the desk of the AP and UPI wire service offices in the city where the speech is delivered.

TV AND RADIO INTERVIEWS

Since the speech is news, the local (place of speech delivery) TV and radio outlets should receive not only printed copies of the speech but a one-page biography of the speaker, a copy of the program (if it exists), or a fact sheet on the who, what, where, when, and why of the speech.

Frequently an interview on the day of the speech will be arranged on the merits of the advance copy of the speech.

REPRINTS IN BOOKLET FORM

An inexpensive reprint of the speech can be produced in a booklet size that will fit the standard business envelope. A brief statement explaining the occasion for the speech should be part of the title page. Also, tell the reader where he can obtain additional copies.

WHO GETS THE BOOKLET?

First, start within your company. Pick out top management and department heads for a starter, but have additional copies available for requestors who are not on the distribution list. People who do not belong on the executive mail list can get sensitive about being "overlooked," and therefore it is well to have some copies on the fringes of top management.

Second, mail the speech reprint to your business and professional peers outside of the company. Mail it to your customers, actual and potential. Mail copies to trade magazines in your field, and the fields related to the speech topic.

Finally, mail the speech booklet to people in the government. Direct it primarily to the federal agencies and departments most closely affected by your remarks. And it will do no harm to mail it to select senators and representatives who are on appropriate committees or who represent your state. And don't overlook state and local government officials. You, as a citizen, have a right to a hearing and a right to let your ideas be known where they may do some good.

You may be happily surprised to see your speech, or excerpts from it, get good press coverage at all levels of communication.

Don't be surprised at what is quoted. Your most dramatic and expressive comments may be overlooked, and some statement you deemed inconsequential may be the quotable quote. It certainly gives you, the speaker, pause for reflection. Still, your words were quoted, and you really did have something to say.

20

THE MORGUE

Artists generally maintain a reference file of illustrations that serve as source material for numerous topics. They call this file "the morgue" —an accurate, though not cheering, label.

The speech writer should start his own "morgue," a reference source for speech material. Setting up the file is easy; the operation and maintenance of a *useful* file call for guides.

ORGANIZATION

First, set aside a separate area for the morgue; divide the area into "general business" and "professional" files. The general business section contains things that touch upon business operation in general but that may affect your work. The professional section contains the material strictly pertinent to your occupation: as a scientist, engineer, doctor, accountant, or a similar profession.

An example will illustrate organization of the file.

As a medical doctor, you would be interested in news of government legislation on Medicare and Medicaid, in a story on a new electronic device to aid in your therapy, or in the public affairs announcements of the American Medical Association. These would be general business items.

The professional file would contain material directly related to your work: a feature story in the *AMA Journal*; a paper delivered at a symposium; the script from an audiovisual presentation you attended; and similar literature.

The general business file has remote utility, to be sure; the professional file is more likely to have current usefulness. Still, the breadth and depth of the respective files will provide a quantity of source material for a given speech. Moreover, a speech should be written in a context, an environment; the "general" file will make it comparatively easy to develop a setting for a narrowly defined speech topic.

CURRENT FILES

Files for the sake of files don't profit the speech writer. There should be a periodic updating; information can become useless. A new discovery, latest results of tests, shifting viewpoints and opinions can make the file information obsolete.

The files should be up-dated at least once a year; continual updating is the ideal goal, but demands on time make this seem unfeasible.

DOCUMENT CONTROL

One document that should be in the morgue is the speech you give. This is quite important if there is a strong probability of future speaking assignments.

Some type of document control is necessary to avoid giving the same speech to the same audience at a later date. This has happened occasionally, but it is more common in religious preaching: some sermons have lived, as is, for years and years. The congregation knows them by heart.

A cover sheet stapled to the speech manuscript will help ensure against forgetfulness. The sheet would contain:

1. Title of speech.
2. Name of audience.
3. Location given.
4. Date given.
5. Your name.
6. Your company.
7. Summary—three-sentence paragraph.
8. Remarks—audience reaction to speech, comments on it, request for copies, etc.

The Summary Check List at the end of this chapter shows a sample format for the cover sheet.

One observation for all speechifiers: Don't be afraid to use the same speech again, or to use parts of it for other speeches. There's nothing wrong with that practice, under the limitations described above, and an awful lot of work is avoided.

SUMMARY CHECK LIST

Sample Format of Cover Sheet

"Senate Spotlight on Ethics"

An Address
to
The Riverboat Chamber of Commerce
Riverboat, Ohio

June 19, 1968

John J. Cosgrove
Vice President—Marketing
Happy-Time Industries, Inc.
New York, New York

Summary: An analysis of ethical standards instituted; enforcement of those standards; state adopting code of ethics.

Remarks: Address published in Riverboat C. of C. magazine; 100 reprints issued at office.

21
AUDIOVISUAL PRESENTATIONS

That hybrid called the audiovisual (A/V) presentation is extremely popular with speakers. The A/V presentation consists of two elements: a written text that serves as a script, and graphic slides to support and emphasize key portions of the text.

The A/V is useful in addressing a small audience of 100 or 200 people, in contrast with a formal speech delivered to an audience three to five times larger. Many speakers prefer the A/V presentation to the formal speech. The A/V is easier to prepare and does not require the public speaking skills used in a formal speech. Also, the A/V can impress an audience more strongly than a speech, since *two* senses (hearing *and* sight) are affected by the presentation.

Various guidelines to presentations and some cautions on the use of A/V's are offered below.

TYPE OF SLIDE

The 35 mm slide is recommended for the A/V graphics. This slide is well suited to high-quality art, color, and illustrations set in a well-designed format, and is quite impressive when projected on a screen.

WRITING THE A/V TEXT

I have been agreeably surprised to find that the presentation text is far easier to write if slide texts and art are prepared first. The slide texts are comparatively easy to define, and they serve well as miniature outlines for writing the text.

The presentation draft should be typed with a two-inch left margin. This allows placement of the slide number on the sideline of the text calling for the slide. Of course, all slides will be numbered before any practice session begins. "Black" slides interleaved with the graphic slides will eliminate the empty white screen when the graphic slide is no longer needed in illustration.

REHEARSING THE PRESENTATION

A dry-run of the presentation is imperative. Timing is important; smooth transition is important; proper arrangement of slides is important. Ideally, the projector operator will be someone other than the speaker. The speaker, who is both presenter and projector, stands an excellent chance of making a sloppy presentation.

CAUTIONS ON A/V PRESENTATIONS

All audiovisual presentations are governed by "Murphy's law." This principle, though not as elevated and incisive as Parkinson's fundamental law, has an earthiness and universality that the Parkinson law lacks.

Murphy's law states: "If anything can possibly go wrong in an audiovisual presentation, it will go wrong."

"A word to the wise" is of little benefit to the person making an audiovisual presentation. Still, the speaker cannot be left to the mercy of the A/V environment.

If at all possible, the speaker should check the location where the presentation is to be given. He should be on the lookout for stray wires on the floor around the speaking area, a screen that will not adjust properly, a rickety projector stand, and a sound system that offers two choices: a high-pitched sound or none at all.

The A/V speaker who uses a company slide projector and a company employee as the operator should insist that emergency supplies be carried by the operator. Two extension cords, two fuses, and two projection bulbs are absolute minimums for survival.

Preparing a formal speech may not be so bad, after all.

TIPS ON SLIDE PREPARATION

There are "do's and don't's" to preparing slides for audiovisual presentations, and a few ideas are offered here to aid the speaker in translating his ideas into effective slides.

FAULTS AND REMEDIES IN SLIDE COMPOSITION

Fault. The most common mistake in preparing slides is trying to tell the whole story of an idea on one slide. Some of these clustered creations look more like an ink blot test than a concise highlighting of a thought.

Remedy. Express the idea in a few essential words, much like the style of a telegram. The topics on a slide are used to focus the attention of the audience; it is still up to the speaker to fleshout those skeletal ideas.

Fault. Using heavily detailed and complex artwork is not only hard on the eyes of the viewer, it is a hindrance to intelligibility.

Remedy. Use a "blow-up" of a portion of the drawing. If necessary, use two or three slides to simplify—and communicate—complex artwork.

Fault. Lack of a standard format for preparation permits handwritten copy, free-hand sketches, printed material, and the like to be used without any regard for slide appearance.

Remedy. Establish a standard format (or, at least, a minimum standard) for displaying ideas on slides, whether it be words or artwork. Use a type style that is easy to read; limit copy to a maximum of three or four lines, plus slide title.

Fault. Artwork—sketches, drawings, photographs, graphs—may vary from crudely amateur to highly professional.

Remedy. Use only good-quality photographs for slide transparencies; have artwork drawn, or redrawn, by a professional. If a number of slides have color, use color as a background for any black-and-white art.

A NOTE ON SLIDE PROJECTION

It is not necessary to keep the audience in complete darkness when projecting. If the lights are dimmed, or the lights near the screen are turned off, it will be easier on the eyes of the audience. To avoid that white splash of light reflecting off the screen when no slide is being shown, interleaf "blank slides" between the regular slides. A "blank" is nothing more than a black cardboard piece inserted in the slide frame.

22

A WORD TO THE
OCCASIONAL SPEAKER

The big day has come and gone; the speech has been given. It seemed well received; applause was hearty, a few people buttonholed you for questions, some even asked for copies of the speech. You have a few nice letters in your file.

But, is that it?

All the time you spent in research, writing, rewriting, rehearsal, polishing, and criticizing—are all those hours of effort just history? That's entirely up to the speech writer.

There are fringe benefits in writing just one speech. Many of the techniques used in speech writing can be utilized in your daily occupation. It's true that "speechifying is a different animal." It's just as true that many speech writing skills apply to expository writing as such.

In his professional world, the writer can turn out superior letters, presentations, proposals, signed feature articles, and perhaps even that long-lost document: a well-written memo.

There are exceedingly few intelligent, meaningful, lean and well-written memos. The man who can start a memo without using "herewith attached" (whatever language that is) will become a journalistic luminary among his colleagues and superiors. The subject of memo writing is worthy of a book!

The professional person who can write without using "legalese" and archaisms might just infect his colleagues with some of his skill; he might tactfully point out some techniques to subordinates. Some "legalese" and archaisms, with English equivalents, are: forthwith (immediately); heretofore (previously); thusly (so); effective as of (effective); hereby designated (named or called); albeit (although); perchance (perhaps); and all other "legalese" and archaisms of that ilk (kind).

The writer who eliminates the sentence starting "In other words" (which explains what the preceeding sentence meant) will be the glory of communications.

So, these chapters in the book should be helpful in prose composition:

Chapter 7   Writing a Lean Speech
Chapter 8   Watch Your Language
Chapter 10   Your Style of Writing
Chapter 12   As You Write (Axioms 3, 4, and 5)
Chapter 13   Criticism (editing, if you like)

The next part of this book, called "Reference," is intended to supplement the writing technique dealt with in Part I.

PART II
REFERENCE

SECTION I SUMMARY CHECK LISTS

For convenience and utility to the reader the Summary Check Lists of Part I have been collected in this section.

SAMPLE OUTLINE (Chapter 6)

Topic: "Automobile Safety"

SECTION I. REVIEW OF CURRENT EVENTS

1.1 Comments of Nader's book
1.2 Testimony of Auto Experts
1.3 Detroit's Reaction
1.1 *Nader's "Unsafe at Any Speed"*
   —background on author
   —examples in book: selective, slanted, sensational
   —engineering qualifications of author
1.2 *Testimony of Experts*
   —engineering directors of "Big Three"
   —safety tests used: brake, impact, suspension
1.3 *Detroit's Reaction*
   —discussion with government agency
   —compliance with standards, generally
   —will increase cost to consumer

WRITING A LEAN SPEECH (Chapter 7)

Trim all verbal fat
Eliminate "nothing" sentences
Use concrete terms
Write tight sentences
Justify adjectives

WATCH YOUR LANGUAGE (Chapter 8)

Eradicate "wise"
Use the appropriate word
Use small words
Avoid jargon
Minimize quotations

YOUR STYLE OF WRITING (Chapter 10)

Avoid passive voice
Use the first-person pronoun
Write spontaneously
Use triads
Vary the pace of writing

ALMOST READY TO WRITE (Chapter 11)

Write a 20-minute speech
Useful skillful repetition
Create environment for speech
Typed page = 2½ minutes speaking time

AS YOU WRITE (Chapter 12)

Write out the speech
Follow the outline
Think paragraphs
Assume nothing
Avoid periodic sentences

THE WRITER AS SPEAKER (Chapter 14)

Speak slowly
Relax to breathe easier

Check voice patterns
Use "cues" in speech

THE WRITER REHEARSES (Chapter 15)

Practice perfectly
Look at audience
Stay in one place
Use gestures
Time your speech

THE INDEX CARD AND YOU (Chapter 17)

—*Senator Jones:* in serious political trouble; he's "dove," constituents are "hawks."
  chance to get back popularity by attacking taxes.
—*Cosgrove's Book:*
    —advertising versus R&D; 4x for ads as R&D
    —ignores contributions of auto makers CGNP & standard of living)
  * —slanted, selective, sensational versions of mistakes
    —cf. *Chicago Tribune* and *Miami Herald* feature stories
—*Public Opinion:*
    —against manufacturers of hardware: $$ additional
    —"bad press" making sensationalism
    —information must come from mfrs.; full program
    nccded

THE MORGUE (Chapter 20)

Sample Format of Cover Sheet

"Senate Spotlight on Ethics"

Riverboat, Ohio
June 19, 1968

John J. Cosgrove
Vice President—Marketing

Happy-Time Industries, Inc.
New York, New York

Summary: An analysis of ethical standards instituted; enforcement of those standards; state adopting code of ethics.

Remarks: Address published in Riverboat C. of C. magazine, 100 reprints issued at office.

SECTION 2   EXERCISES IN LEAN WRITING

There is no "one" way to rewrite the three exercises in this section. The reader may write versions that differ from mine, provided that he reduces loose, wordy writing to trim proportions. Editing and rewriting may be done in the text.

The exercises are authentic excerpts, but I have modified them slightly.

Exercise I

1   One of the most common of the emotional disorders is schizo-

2   phrenia which disease scientists have studied for years. Heretofore,

3   studies were undertaken with the feeling that any research of the brain

4   had to have a practical application. The fact of the matter is, that

5   now such studies are considered to have value all in themselves. Hence,

6   new drugs, helping us to study the possible effects of chemical imbalance

7   in the brain, have reduced mental hospital wards considerably, in most

8   instances. In other words, further research may discover a cure for

9   schizophrenia.

Exercise I Corrected

Schizophrenia is a most common emotional disorder; scientists have studied the disease for years. Previous studies of this mental disorder assumed that brain research must have practical application. Now, such studies are considered valuable in themselves. New drugs help study the possible effects of chemical imbalance in the brain. These drugs have reduced patient rolls an average of 29.6 percent in 80 of the 100 hospitals tested. Further research may discover a cure for schizophrenia.

Critical Comment on Exercise 1

1   12 words before main idea "schizophrenia" is reached = wordiness

2   "Heretofore" is "legalese"

3   "have been undertaken" = were made

3   "research of the brain" = brain research

4   "had to have" = must have

4   "the fact of the matter is" = simply state the "fact"

5   "studies are considered to have value all in themselves" = are considered valuable in themselves

5   "hence;" who says "hence"?

7   "reduced considerably" = a "nothing" expression; give a fact

8   "in most instances" = zero; need a fact

8   "in other words" = my previous statement is not clear

Exercise II

1   I would like to say that these men could be called the builders

2   of our city, not that they actually built buildings, but that they decided

3   what buildings, facilities, renovations, et cetera were mostly need to

4   get the city on the ball again. It was, in the year 1947, their fore-sight

5   which made them sit down to plan to build all those marvelous things. They

6   indeed assembled together, in one fell swoop, such men as might be of in-

7   fluence in the renovation of the city. They needed men, time and wherewith-

8   al. Initially, at the outset of the campaign, these bridge builders, as it

9   were, decided that the cooperation of the press, always in prox-imity

10   with the public pulse, should consider public cooperation to be of pressing

11   moment.

Exercise II   Corrected

I suggest we call these men "the planners of our city." They alone decided what buildings, facilities, and renewals were most needed to get this city moving again.

In 1947, these men of foresight planned the construction of all those marvelous buildings: the library, the civic center, and the hospi-tal. Influential citizens were invited to assist in planning the renova-tion.

The planners needed men, time, and money. They also knew that newspaper support was important; the press feels the public pulse, and public enthusiasm was urgently needed.

Critical Comment

1 "I would like . . . could be called" = I suggest we call

1 "the builders" = planners; following clause says they did not build

2 "not that they actually built buildings" = delete the clause; it explains what is *not* meant by "builders of our city"

3 "et cetera" = what "things?" Omit the expression

3 "mostly needed" = "most" is the adverb

4 "in 1947" = out of place in sentence, relocate

5 "to plan to build" = to plan the construction

5 "all those marvelous things" = what things? Marvelous is a strong adjective to describe things

6 "in one fell swoop" = Oh prithee and forsooth; drop it

6 "as might be" = subjunctive; make indicative

7 "wherewithal" = money, or financing

8 "Initially, at the outset" = redundancy

8 "these bridge builders" = we agreed they were not bridge builders

8 "as it were" = he apologizes for previous expression; delete

9 "in close proximity" = "he's tall for his height"; delete "close"

10 "should consider . . . pressing moment" = "beating around the bush"; see corrected exercise

10 "of pressing moment" = contrived expression, un-natural speech; means urgent, important

Exercise III

1 Immediately the contract is awarded, qualified personnel,

2 trained for the job, will be installed at the tracking station. In

3   building the display console, workmanlike construction will be
used,

4   the command console will have a "black box" as the monitor of all

5   equipment. The equipment used will be of high grade, with quality

6   components utilized throughout. The contractor feels that additional

7   economies and high utility will occur when the specified system is

8   integrated. Operationswise, the program should lead to high optimi-

9   zation of activities, and further efficiency is to be looked forward to.

Exercise III   Corrected

When the contract is awarded, installation specialists will be sent
to the tracking station, to build the specified console.

All equipment and components will meet or exceed the specified
quality standards; in addition, a classified device on the command
console will monitor all equipment.

In the proposed system, the contractor can effect a six-percent
reduction in annual maintenance costs, while operating the equipment for three shifts, instead of two.

Critical Comment

1   "Immediately the" = British English; means "when" or "if"

1   "qualified personnel" = would unqualified personnel be used?

2   "installed" = for university president, yes; worker, no

3   "workmanlike" = but, they won't really be workers; they'll just act
like workmen

4   "black box" = jargon; use proper term

4   "as the monitor of" = to monitor

5   "feels" = who cares how he feels; use guarantee, assures, offers, and so forth

6   "additional economies" = 0

7   "high utility" = 0

8   "Operationswise" = "suffixitis," advanced stages; delete

8   "optimization" = flapdoodle

9   "is to be looked forward to" = is expected

SECTION 3   FIGURES OF SPEECH

The speech writer can make good use of these techniques to heighten the effect of his words. There is one caution: he should not force the use of these figures or try to use all of them in one speech. Instead, let the writer become thoroughly familiar with these figures. Their use will be suggested to him as the speech is being written.

Alliteration

Alliteration is the deliberate and noticeable use of a series of words beginning with or containing the same letter or sound.

"Successful speech writers seriously study speakers."

"His pride was lashed, his ambitions were smashed, his hopes were dashed."

And whoever forgot: "Peter Piper picked a peck of pickled peppers," which has both initial and internal alliteration?

Anaphora

Anaphora is the marked repetition of a word or phrase in successive clauses or phrases. It makes use of the triad.

"The engine coughed, it sputtered, it died."

"I came, I saw, I conquered."

"We shall fight on the beaches . . . We shall fight on the landing grounds . . . We shall fight in the fields . . ."

Brachylogy

The term means "short speech."

"Less talk, more work."
("Let there be less talk" . . . etc.)

"No tickee, no washee."
(If you don't have a ticket, you don't get your laundry.)

"Some chicken. Some neck."
(Churchill commenting on Hitler's remark that he would handle England just as you wring a chicken's neck.)

Chiasmus

Literally, chiasmus means "in the form of the Greek χ;" the balanced components of a sentence are marched one above the other and connected by diagonal lines; $X = X$.

"Ask not what your country can do for you, but rather, what you can do for your country."

Hendiadys

Means "one through two." One expression is understood as applying to the second.

"Try and do better." (Try to do better.)

"To cease and desist." (To cease and to desist.)

Although not "proper" English, I suggest that it is a natural evolution, and soon will be acceptable usage: try and stop it.

Hyperbole

The term means "overthrowing;" the Greeks really do have a word for everything. Hyperbole is nothing more than exaggeration for the sake of emphasis.

"I told him a million times not to go there."

"Every policeman must now be a legal expert."

Litotes

The explanation of such obvious usage is complicated. Litotes means that a positive idea is obtained by substituting the opposite idea with a negative.

"She's *no* spring chicken." (She's old.)

"I am a citizen of *no* mean country." (Famous country.)

"Not bad, huh?" (Quite good, yes?)

Metonymy

The substitution of an attributive or other suggestive word.

"The *Administration* asked for new taxes." (President.)

"The Sultan of Swat." (Babe Ruth.)

"Disneyland, East." (Washington, D.C.)

Onomatopoeia

Literally, making a name; the sound is the name.

"The planes zoomed low." (Zoom = sound of planes.)

"Oof! Pow! Crash!" (Batman.)

Rhetorical Question

Instead of making a straight declarative statement, the speaker phrases his thought as a question. The question is strictly for dramatic effect, and no answer is expected or made.

Statement. "No one denies that men love their country."
Rhetorical Question. "Who will deny that men love their country?"

Statement. "A man can ask no more."
Rhetorical Question. "What more can a man ask?"

Synechdoche

The mention of a part for the whole, or vice versa.

"The United States won its second Olympic gold medal."
(The U.S. *basketball team* won.)

"Red sails in the sunset."
(Sails of a *ship*)

SECTION 4   SYMBOLS FOR MARKING COPY

The list of symbols in "printer's shorthand" is adopted for marking copy. They are invaluable tools for anyone who writes, and most professional occupations demand writing: reports, memos, letters, as well as speeches.

Have your secretary copy the symbols and meanings from the book for her own use. A page of edited copy is included here to show application of the symbols.

⊏ = move to the left

⊐ = move to the right

≡ = upper case, capitals

/ = lower case (through a letter)

∧ = insert here

No ¶ = no paragraph indention

¶ = indent a paragraph

Insert = marked where new copy is to be inserted

⌒ = close up word

ℓ = delete word or letter

ℯ = delete and close up

⌣⌐ = transpose, reverse order

⌁ = this matter follows after

≣ = cross out word completely

\# = make a space between

Corrected Typed Copy

Speechwriting is not an easy task. Every speechwriter knows that
writing, research and outlining are the logical order of work. The first task is re-

search. The writer must compile whatever sources he can locate.

No ¶ And the sources must be current, and accurate.

(INSERT P. 4)

¶ The outline is the key to the speech.

[The outline has been called the measure of the speech writer.
And that statement has much merit.

Even in such an extreme example as this, much repetitive writing

of corrections is avoided.

SECTION 5   MISTAKES IN GRAMMAR

"Ain't I the one with the *A* in the final exam?" the student asked his
teacher. "Ain't I?" barked the teacher. "Aren't I," replied the student.
Both persons nodded, both agreed. Both were wrong.

"Ain't," at least, is based on a reasonable premise that it is a contraction for "I am not," which is a correct verb form.

"Aren't," which is supposed to be correct, is a contraction of "I are not," a form that no one has ever seen in English grammar.

These remarks give a fair picture of the state of English grammar today. Grammar is determined by usage. Many people, however, think that what they know and use is usage and therefore is correct grammar.

The grammarians—the ones who established the rules of English grammar—determine not just usage, but they also specify "acceptable" usage. A number of helpful grammars are listed in Section 7 of this part. The discussion of grammar in this chapter is limited to the common grammatical failings that occur in speech writing. These are dangling participles, incorrect use of moods, and incorrect use of "that" and "which."

The Dangling Participle

The dangling participle expression is a grammatical failing that is quite common, frequently comic, and constantly repeated. It takes careful writing to avoid the dangling participle, called so because there is no word that can serve as subject for the participle.

The textile executive who wrote "Being a salesman in the automobile business, I know you are concerned with the merger of your company into ours, and what your future may be," actually identified himself as an automobile salesman, which he was not. A few replies to his letter informed him of that fact.

The most common example of the dangling participle is: "Barking and growling ferociously, I saw the dog heading my way." Surely the writer doesn't mean that.

What he means to say, or at least his thought is, "I saw a barking and ferociously growling dog heading my way." If the original statement of the writer is true, we can assume that the dog was mystified, if not frightened, at the man's behavior.

Notice that the dangling participle is prevalent in so-called technical writing. Its use in engineering, science, and related technical disciplines is not always so obvious, nor so humorous, as the previous example.

There is only one way for the speech writer to avoid the dangling participle. He must critically evaluate his thought before he puts it on paper. It's that simple—and that difficult.

If the dangling participle construction gets into his speech text, the writer can catch it in his review of the first draft. And, the person who reviews the speech will also have an opportunity to cite the usage.

Incorrect Use of Moods

The moods of the language are indicative, imperative, subjunctive and infinitive. The subjunctive and infinitive moods, which are in grammatical flux, are sometimes poorly used by writers.

Usage of the subjunctive mood is properly limited to "if . . . were" clauses: "If I were president," and so forth.

Unfortunately, speech writers persist in using the "learned" subjunctive mood, even though the indicative now replaces the subjunctive.

"If that were true, I would not make the statement" is certainly subjunctive, but present-day usage calls for "If that *was* true. . . ." It may cause a few linguistic shudders, but "was" is correct.

It is safe to state that the speech writer should almost *always* substitute indicative for subjunctive.

The Infinitive

The infinitive, which is both a verbal noun and a mood, has been a hybrid. For some reason writers feel that the infinitive of purpose is not strong enough by itself, and they prop it up with a few unnecessary speech particles.

The words that introduce a clause are placed before the infinitive to show purpose. "In order" plus the infinitive is the usual shape of the mood.

The probable reason for the "in-order-to" construction is seen in the following example. "She sent the money in order that (or so that) he might buy the machine" contains a subordinate clause construction that is so unwieldy that we naturally and easily substitute "money to buy the machine."

In the example, "In order to buy," the expression is grammatically incorrect for two reasons: First, the infinitive *per se* expresses purpose; second, "in order" is used to introduce a clause with a finite verb; that is, one with inflected endings. The infinitive is not inflected. The infinitive by itself will express purpose.

"That" and "Which"

A maxim of the scholastics states: "When the doctors disagree, the student is free." This adage is a good note on which to start the discussion of "that" and "which."

That and which are relative pronouns; the former is called restrictive, the latter is called nonrestrictive. And once this statement has been made, the dispute begins. The sharp distinction between "that" and "which" is frequently overlooked. A common usage of one term does not exist. So the speech writer may write what he pleases, but he is urged to reflect on the differences between the two pronouns.

The restrictive pronoun "that" limits the meaning of the the noun it modifies. In the example, "I took the manuscript that the manager had edited," "that" introduces a restrictive clause. Removing the restrictive clause completely changes the thought content of the sentence.

In the example, "He used the new formula, which he had verified himself, to compute the trajectory," the "which" clause is nonrestrictive; it only adds an accidental quality to the substantial thought: "new formula to compute."

SUMMARY CHECK LIST

Eliminate dangling participles
Avoid subjunctive
Use infinitive properly
Distinguish "that" and "which"

SECTION 6 PUNCTUATION

Punctuation is important to the speech writer, the speech, and the speaker. Some of the more important "do's and don'ts" are discussed. The subject of punctuation is not a closed issue; new methods of punctuation are creeping into the speech writing business.

The punctuation symbols considered here are the comma, semi-colon, colon, quotation, ellipsis and dash, and exclamation point. The period and question mark are self-explanatory.

The Comma

Use the comma only when you absolutely have to, avoid its use wherever possible. The comma slows down the action in a sentence. A writer who is "comma happy" does not write well.

Certain uses of the comma are recommended.

Use a comma before the conjunction connecting the two parts of a compound sentence. If the writer says, "Calculating market shares and rising prices, and a quarterly dividend yet to be paid," and omits the comma after "prices," the reader will trip on the first reading, go back and reread, and perhaps still not be sure of the meaning.

Use a comma in a lengthy sentence when you think the speaker will need a pause, either for meaning or breathing.

Short phrases and some adverbs at the beginning of the sentence can be run into the sentence without a comma for a pause: "In this case you are right"; or "Perhaps he will return."

In a series of three or more items, place a comma before the conjunction. The comma may be necessary and it seems to place equal emphasis on all words in the series. I feel that the omission of the comma weakens the force of the series.

In the sentence, "The estate is to be divided among Tom, Dick and Harry," Tom gets half of the estate, Dick and Harry each get a quarter. If the series read Tom, Dick, and Harry, they would each get one third.

In the example, "We need men, machines and money" I feel that there is greater emphasis and heightened effect if the series read, "men, machines, and money."

The Semicolon

The semicolon is used to show both the omission of a conjunction and a change in thought within a sentence: "He took the car from father; he took the checkbook from mother."

The semicolon is quite useful in clarifying necessarily involved concepts. "The first series of equations were plotted by hand; the second were run on a computer."

The Colon

The colon has one function; it introduces what immediately follows: "This is the reason for our existence: profit."

Quotation Marks

The use of quotation marks is the source of some bitter feuding among speech writers. Decide on one method of treatment and stick to it. The simplest solution is to put all punctuation inside the quotation marks. The solution is quick, neat, and provocative.

Ellipsis and Dash

The ellipsis (three dots in a series) is becoming a punctuation tool for many speech writers. It is difficult to understand why. The ellipsis asks for a mental assumption on the part of the reader or listener. In the sentence, "We have a new controller . . . a man of vast experience . . . one who will help our company . . ." the dots stand for something, but it is difficult to tell what.

The three dots seem to indicate that the writer does not have command of his thought, or at least he cannot express it. The ellipsis is a valid punctuation mark when used sparingly and deliberately; otherwise it becomes a crutch to bolster poor skills.

The dash is also a favorite tool of some speech writers. The dash is a solid line of dots substituted for the three dots. Some speeches use both words *and* Morse code.

The speech writer should avoid these two devices. Period.

Exclamation Point

Avoid the use of exclamation points in punctuation. Let both words and speaker do the exclaiming. Actually, the exclamation point comes too late in the sentence to cue an emotion.

The Spanish language rather cleverly, or logically, inverts exclamation points and question marks before the sentence to signal the reader as to what follows.

But we are dealing with English-sentence punctuation. The skillful writer does not need the exclamation point. Moreover, the use of this mark seems to be quite uncommon today.

SECTION 7 BASIC LIBRARY FOR SPEECH WRITERS

The books listed here are basic reference books for speech writing (and for written communications in general). These basic books are only a foundation: additional books for the writer are discussed under the heading "More Books for the Library."

Basic Books

The New Roget's Thesaurus, edited by Norman Lewis. Garden City, New York: Garden City Books Edition, 1961. Copyright 1961, G. P. Putnam's. 552 pp. This book is a "must" for writers; the new dictionary form is quite helpful. One caution for inexperienced writers: choosing the precise word will demand careful thought.

Webster's Third New International Dictionary of the English Language, Springfield, Mass.: G. and C. Merriam Company, 1961. A generally excellent work, and an authoritative source for the writer, in spite of criticism from reactionary reviewers.

Familiar Quotations, by John Bartlett. Boston: Little, Brown and Company, 1955. 1614 pp. The book is indispensable to find the *correct* version of a quotation; it is amazing how many familiar and commonly accepted quotations are inaccurate.

English Grammar, by George O. Curme. New York: Barnes & Noble, 1966. 308 pp. This book is a paperback in the publisher's College Outline Series; treatment of grammar is excellent and thorough.

The Elements of Style, by William Strunk, Jr. New York: The Macmillan Company, 1959. 71 pp.

The professor has written a witty and intelligent bestseller; he and Fowler (see next heading) have turned out lucid and interesting writing on the business of writing.

More Books for the Library

DICTIONARIES

A Dictionary of Modern English Usage, by H. W. Fowler. New York: Oxford University Press, 1944. 742 pp.

Random House Dictionary of the English Language, by Random House, 1966. 2059 pp. Some reviews were quite caustic; the book is quite useful, but Strunk and Fowler would have delighted in reviewing it.

Webster's Seventh New Collegiate Dictionary, Springfield, Mass., G. and C. Merriam Company, 1965. 1221 pp. Based on *Third New International,* the book is handy; i.e., the writer will ordinarily not choose to hand the larger dictionary from office to home, and vice versa.

GRAMMARS

An Advanced English Grammar, by George Lyman Kittredge and Frank Edgar Farley. Boston: Ginn and Company, 1913. 333 pp. The best English grammar ever written, period.

MANUALS OF STYLE

A Manual of Style (containing typographical and other rules for authors, recommended by the University of Chicago Press, together with specimens of type). Chicago: The University of Chicago, Eleventh Edition, 1949. 534 pp. As you might judge from the title, the *Manual* is primarily intended for scholars and university publications. Only certain sections of the book will interest the speech writer; the *Manual* is considered to be the "classic" in its field, and some notice of it is necessary.

Watch Your Language, Theodore M. Bernstein. New York: Pocket Books, 1966. 213 pp. Bernstein, assistant managing editor of *The New York Times,* writes for newspaper writers. His comments, though, are quite useful for "tight" writing, a goal suggested for the speech writer.

Style Book of The New York Times, New York: The New York Times Company, 1956. 102 pp. and Supplement. A small loose-leaf book of interesting style tips, and also a reliable guide, much imitated by writers.

PUBLIC SPEAKING BOOKS

The following books treat public speaking in detail, with some emphasis on the technical-scientific aspects. Any one of the three books will be helpful.

Dynamic Public Speaking, George M. Glasgow. New York: Harper and Row, 1950, 315 pp.

How to Speak Effectively on All Occasions, George W. Hibbitt. New York: Perma Giants, 1949. 308 pp.

You Can Talk Well, Richard C. Reager (revised by Norman P. Crawford and Edwin L. Stevens), Rutgers University Press, 1960. 212 pp.

PART III

DIRECTORY OF INFORMATION SOURCES

This section contains 45 general categories that should prove useful as information sources for speech material. The topics were selected on the broad basis of probable influence on speech subjects.

Requests for information should be addressed to the Director of Public Relations or, in the case of the Government, to the Director of Public Information.

Aerospace Industries Association of America
1725 De Sales Street, N.W.
Washington, D.C. 20036

American Institute of Aeronautics and Astronautics
1290 Avenue of the Americas
New York, New York 10019

National Business Aircraft Association
401 Pennsylvania Building, N.W.
Washington, D.C. 20004

Federal Aviation Agency
800 Independence Avenue, S.W.
Washington, D.C. 20553

National Aeronautics and Space Administration
Washington, D.C. 20546

AUTOMOBILES

Automobile Manufacturers' Association, Inc.
320 New Center Building
Detroit, Michigan 48202

Automotive Safety Foundation
200 Ring Building
1200—18th Street, N.W.
Washington, D.C. 20036

Society of Automotive Engineers
485 Lexington Avenue
New York, New York 10017

BANKING (AND FINANCE)

American Bankers Association
90 Park Avenue
New York, New York 10016

Bank Public Relations & Marketing Association
120 West Madison Street
Chicago, Illinois 60602

Foundation for Commercial Banks
Philadelphia National Bank Building
Philadelphia, Pennsylvania 19107

Federal Reserve System
20th Street and Constitution Avenue, N.W.
Washington, D.C. 20551

115

BUSINESS

Business Council
888—17th Street, N.W.
Washington, D.C. 20006

National Associated Businessmen, Inc.
100 Connecticut Avenue, N.W.
Washington, D.C. 20036

National Federation of Independent Business
150 West 20th Avenue
San Mateo, California 94402

Department of Commerce
Director of Publications and Information
14th Street—between Constitution Ave. and E Street, N.W.
Washington, D.C. 20230

CHEMICALS

American Chemical Society
1155 16th Street, N.W.
Washington, D.C. 20036

Chemical Public Relations Association, Inc.
56 West 45th Street
New York, New York 10017

COMPUTERS (AND DATA PROCESSING)

Association for Computing Machinery
211 East 43rd Street
New York, New York 10017

Data Processing Management Association
505 Busse Highway
Park Ridge, Illinois 60068

Systems & Procedures Association
7890 Brookside Drive
Cleveland, Ohio 44138

General Services Administration
18th and "F" Streets, N.W.
Washington, D.C. 20405

DRUGS (PHARMACEUTICALS)

Pharmaceutical Manufacturers Association
1155 15th Street, N.W.
Washington, D.C. 20005

Food and Drug Administration
U.S. Department of Health, Education and Welfare
200 "C" Street, S.W.
Washington, D.C. 20024

ECONOMICS

American Economics Association
Northwestern University
629 Noyes Street
Chicago, Illinois 60201

National Association of Business Economists
P.O. Box 2804
Washington, D.C. 20013

Office of Business Economics
Department of Commerce
14th Street—between Constitution Ave. and E Street, N.W.
Washington, D.C. 20230

EDUCATION

National Education Association of the United States
1201—16th Street
Washington, D.C. 20036

National School Public Relations Association
1201—16th Street
Washington, D.C. 20036

National Science Teachers Association
1201—16th Street
Washington, D.C. 20036

Department of Health, Education and Welfare
330 Independence Avenue, S.W.
Washington, D.C. 20201

ELECTRONICS AND ELECTRICITY

Institute of Electrical and Electronics Engineers
345 East 47th Street
New York, New York 10017

Government information sources are varied, consult by topic: TVA, Bonneville Power Administration, marketing, export, import, and so forth.

EMPLOYMENT

Bureau of Labor Statistics
Department of Labor

14th Street and Constitution Avenue, N.W.
Washington, D.C. 20210

ENGINEERING (NOT ELECTRONIC OR ELECTRICAL)

There are about 60; consult the field of specialty for information.

American Association of Engineers
8 South Michigan Boulevard
Chicago, Illinois 60603

National Science Foundation
Engineering Division
1800 G Street, N.W.
Washington, D.C. 20550

Consult also the engineering bureaus and divisions of various Government Departments.

FARMS (AND FARM EQUIPMENT)

American Farm Bureau Federation
1000 Merchandise Mart
Chicago, Illinois 60654

Farm Equipment Manufacturers Association
Suite 710
230 South Bemiston
St. Louis, Missouri 63105

Department of Agriculture
14th Street and Independence Avenue, S.W.
Washington, D.C. 20250

FOREIGN TRADE

American Chamber of Commerce Executives
Suite 806
1522 "K" Street, N.W.
Washington, D.C. 20005

National Foreign Trade Council, Inc.
10 Rockefeller Plaza
New York, New York 10020

Society for International Development
1346 Connecticut Avenue, N.W.
Washington, D.C. 20036

Department of Commerce
Bureau of International Commerce
14th Street—between Constitution Ave. and E Street, N.W.
Washington, D.C. 20230

FUELS

Coal

National Coal Association
1130—17th Street, N.W.
Washington, D.C. 20036

Gas

American Gas Association
605 Third Avenue
New York, New York 10016

Petroleum

American Petroleum Institute
1271 Avenue of the Americas
New York, New York 10020

Department of Interior
C Street—between 18th and 19th Streets, N.W.
Washington, D.C. 20240

HEALTH

National Health Federation
211 West Colorado Boulevard
Monrovia, California 91016

Department of Health, Education and Welfare
330 Independence Avenue, S.W.
Washington, D.C. 20201

HEALTH (PUBLIC)

American Public Health Association
1790 Broadway
New York, New York 10019

United States Public Health Service
Department of Health, Education and Welfare
330 Independence Avenue, S.W.
Washington, D.C. 20201

INSURANCE

Insurance Information Institute
110 William Street
New York, New York 10038

Institute of Life Insurance
277 Park Avenue
New York, New York 10017

Consult proper title: Federal Deposit, veterans, old age, social security, and the life, for Government insurance information.

LAW

American Bar Association
1155 East 60th Street
Chicago, Illinois 60637

American Law Institute
101 North 33rd Street
Philadelphia, Pennsylvania 19104

Federal Bar Association
1815 "H" Street, N.W.
Washington, D.C. 20006

Law Librarian
Library of Congress
First Street S.E.—between East Capitol St. and Independence Ave.
Washington, D.C. 20540

MACHINERY

Associated Equipment Distributors
615 West 22nd Street
Oak Brook, Illinois 60523

Machinery & Allied Products Institute
1200—18th Street, N.W.
Washington, D.C. 20036

MARKETING

American Marketing Association
230 North Michigan Avenue
Chicago, Illinois 60601

MATHEMATICS

American Mathematical Society
P.O. Box 6248
Providence, Rhode Island 02904

Institute of Mathematical Statistics
Department of Statistics
University of North Carolina
Chapel Hill, North Carolina 27515

National Academy of Sciences
2101 Constitution Avenue, N.W.
Washington, D.C. 20418

MEDICINE

American Medical Association
535 North Dearborn Street
Chicago, Illinois 60610

American Psychological Association
1200—17th Street, N.W.
Washington, D.C. 20036

Bureau of Medicine
Food and Drug Administration
200 "C" Street, S.W.
Washington, D.C. 20024

METALS

American Society for Metals
Metals Park, Ohio 44073

Metallurgical Society of AIME
345 East 47th Street
New York, New York 10017

NUCLEAR POWER (ATOMIC ENERGY)

American Nuclear Society
244 East Ogden Avenue
Hinsdale, Illinois 60521

Atomic Energy Commission
1717 H Street, N.W.
Washington, D.C. 20545

OFFICE EQUIPMENT

Business Equipment Manufacturers Association
Room 620, Pfizer Building
235 East 42nd Street
New York, New York 10017

National Office Machine Dealers Association
259 East Devon Avenue
Des Plaines, Illinois 60018

National Stationary & Office Equipment Association
740 Investment Building
Washington, D.C. 20005

PAPER

American Paper Institute
122 East 42nd Street
New York, New York 10017

National Paper Trade Association, Inc.
220 East 42nd Street
New York, New York 10017

PHYSICS

American Institute of Physics
335 East 45th Street
New York, New York 10017

American Physical Society
335 East 45th Street
New York, New York 10017

National Academy of Sciences
2101 Constitution Avenue, N.W.
Washington, D.C. 20418

PRESS

American Newspaper Publishers Association
750 Third Avenue
New York, New York 10017

Associated Press
50 Rockefeller Plaza
New York, New York 10020

United Press International
220 East 42nd Street
New York, New York 10017

United States Information Agency
1750 Pennsylvania Avenue, N.W.
Washington, D.C. 20547

RADIO

National Association of Broadcasters
1771 "N" Street, N.W.
Washington, D.C. 20036

Federal Communications Commission
Post Office Department Building
Washington, D.C. 20554

RAILROADS

Association of American Railroads
Room 640
815—17th Street, N.W.
Washington, D.C. 20006

Railroad Public Relations Association
843 Transportation Building
Washington, D.C. 20006

Railway Progress Institute
38 South Dearborn Street
Chicago, Illinois 60603

Bureau of Railroad Safety and Service
Interstate Commerce Commission
12th Street and Constitution Avenue, N.W.
Washington, D.C. 20423

SALES

Sales and Marketing Executives, International
630 Third Avenue
New York, New York 10017

SCIENCES

American Academy of Arts and Sciences
280 Newton Street
Brooklyn, Massachusetts 02146

National Science Foundation
1800 G Street, N.W.
Washington, D.C. 20550

SHIPS

American Bureau of Shipping
45 Broad Street
New York, New York 10004

American Maritime Association
17 Battery Place
New York, New York 10004

Shipbuilders Council of America
1730 "K" Street, N.W.
Washington, D.C. 20006

Maritime Administration
General Accounting Office Building
441 G Street, N.W.
Washington, D.C. 20235

SOCIOLOGY

American Sociological Association
1001 Connecticut Avenue, N.W.
Washington, D.C. 20036

Division of Social Sciences
National Science Foundation
1800 G Street, N.W.
Washington, D.C. 20550

STEEL (AND IRON)

American Iron and Steel Institute
150 East 42nd Street
New York, New York 10017

STOCK MARKET

American Stock Exchange
86 Trinity Place
New York, New York 10006

New York Stock Exchange
11 Wall Street
New York, New York 10005

Securities and Exchange Commission
500 North Capitol Street, N.W.
Washington, D.C. 20549

TAXATION

Federation of Tax Administrators
1313 East 60th Street
Chicago, Illinois 60637

Tax Executives Institute
1111 "E" Street, N.W.
Washington, D.C. 20004

Internal Revenue Service
15th Street and Pennsylvania Avenue, N.W.
Washington, D.C. 20220

TELEVISION (TV)

National Academy of Television Arts & Sciences
54 West 40th Street
New York, New York 10018

Federal Communications Commission
Post Office Department Building
Washington, D.C. 20554

TRANSPORTATION

Transportation Association of America

1101—17th Street, N.W.
Washington, D.C. 20036

Department of Transportation

TRAVEL

American Travel Association
P.O. Box 347
Appleton, Wisconsin 54911

Travel Research Association
757 Third Avenue
New York, New York 10017

UTILITIES

Gas

American Public Gas Association
734—15th Street, N.W.
Washington, D.C. 20005

Power

American Public Power Association
919—18th Street, N.W.
Washington, D.C. 20006

Water

American Water Works Association, Inc.
2 Park Avenue
New York, New York 10016

Federal Power Commission
General Accounting Office Building
441 "G" Street, N.W.
Washington, D.C. 20426

WELFARE

Child Welfare League of America, Inc.
44 East 23rd Street
New York, New York 10010

Department of Health, Education and Welfare
330 Independence Avenue, S.W.
Washington, D.C. 20201

WOOD

American Forestry Association
919—17th Street, N.W.
Washington, D.C. 20036

Forest Products Research Society
417 North Walnut Street
Madison, Wisconsin 53705

Forest Service
Department of Agriculture
14th Street and Independence Avenue, S.W.
Washington, D.C. 20250

INDEX

FEB 13 1969